Pastor Jim Raley is a dear friend as well as an anointed pastor. I encourage you to read his book *Dream Killers*, because it will challenge and inspire you to keep dreaming your God-given dreams until they become reality. This teaching from the life of Joseph will cause you to look at your circumstances differently and recognize the people and situations that try to steal, kill, and destroy your dreams. It's a message close to my heart as founder of the Dream Center. We chose that name for the center because I wholeheartedly believe that God can help anyone overcome the most incredible obstacles as He restores and fulfills their dreams. If you want to achieve God's purpose for your life and live your dreams, you need to read this book!

—Tommy Barnett
Senior pastor of Phoenix First Assembly
and founder of Los Angeles Dream Center

DREAM
KILLERS

DREAM KILLERS

JIM RALEY

CHARISMA
HOUSE

Most CHARISMA HOUSE BOOK GROUP products are available at special quantity discounts for bulk purchase for sales promotions, premiums, fund-raising, and educational needs. For details, write Charisma House Book Group, 600 Rinehart Road, Lake Mary, Florida 32746, or telephone (407) 333-0600.

DREAM KILLERS by Jim Raley
Published by Charisma House
Charisma Media/Charisma House Book Group
600 Rinehart Road
Lake Mary, Florida 32746
www.charismahouse.com

Unless otherwise noted, all Scripture quotations are from the New King James Version of the Bible. Copyright © 1979, 1980, 1982 by Thomas Nelson, Inc., publishers. Used by permission.

Scripture quotations marked AMP are from the Amplified Bible. Old Testament copyright ©1965, 1987 by the Zondervan Corporation. The Amplified New Testament copyright ©1954, 1958, 1987 by the Lockman Foundation. Used by permission.

Scripture quotations marked KJV are from the King James Version of the Bible.

Scripture quotations marked NAS are from the New American Standard Bible, copyright ©1960, 1962, 1963, 1968, 1971, 1972, 1973, 1975, 1977, 1995 by The Lockman Foundation. Used by permission. (www.Lockman.org)

Scripture quotations marked NIV are from the Holy Bible, New International Version. Copyright © 1973, 1978, 1984, International Bible Society. Used by permission.

Cover design by Justin Evans
Design Director: Bill Johnson

Visit the author's website at www.calvaryfl.com.

Library of Congress Cataloging-in-Publication Data:
An application to register this book for cataloging has been submitted to the Library of Congress.
International Standard Book Number: 978-1-62136-288-3
E-book ISBN: 978-1-62136-289-0

While the author has made every effort to provide accurate telephone numbers and Internet addresses at the time of publication, neither the publisher nor the author assumes any responsibility for errors or for changes that occur after publication.

First edition

13 14 15 16 17 — 9 8 7 6 5 4 3 2 1
Printed in the United States of America

For my dad—the biggest dreamer I ever knew,
a sweet soul, and love on wheels. I miss you,
my precious buddy, and yes, I'm still dreaming!

Contents

Acknowledgments

THANKS SO MUCH TO THE INCREDIBLE CHURCH FAMILY OF Calvary; I'm blessed to lead the most awesome group of dreamers on the planet!

To my friends at Charisma House: thank you, thank you, thank you! You have helped me discover the writer God has called me to be. Every book is a dream awakened.

To my precious family—Dawn, Courtney, Channing, and Peyton: every time I look into your eyes I know without a doubt that the greatest dreams really do come true!

And to every DREAM KILLER in my life that caused me to dream beyond where I was: thank you! I'm still here, and I'm still dreaming... BIG!

Introduction

I HAVE HEARD IT SAID THAT NO PERSON LIVES ABOVE HIS OR her dream. Everybody needs a dream because there is something life giving in it. A dream sustains the soul the way food sustains the body. It's a tragic thing to live with a starving soul.

This book is soul food.

A dream apart from God can often seem mystical and magical, something so distant and farfetched it's almost unattainable. But everything changes when your dream comes from God.

God-sized dreams in the beginning seem impossible and improbable, but eventually they become inevitable. These dreams are incredible because they are not manifested by chance; they are manifested by choice. God chooses to give them, and you choose to dream them. This great big God has designed great big dreams for everyone at every stage of life. He has left no one out, not even you!

God designed and created you to not only dream but also to dream big. Every time you dream big, you are practicing and dress rehearsing your future. It important to realize that if God gave you a dream, then He is for you and for your dream. And if God is for you, and He is for your dream, who can stand against you?

You must never be surprised or alarmed to discover that when your dream is stirred within you, your dream killers are stirred against you. Every dreamer has to deal with dream killers. Dream killers are often disguised as situations, circumstances, close friends, or even family members. It can be your past, your pride, your fear, or even yourself. Regardless of the who or the what, you're about to be equipped with the how in overcoming every dream killer of life.

In the pages of this book you will discover the power of a dream, learning firsthand from one of the greatest dreamers in history, Joseph. If you have never read his story, I encourage you to look it up in your Bible. You can find it in the Book of Genesis, beginning in chapter 37 and ending in chapter 50. Joseph never allowed his circumstances to stop him from dreaming big and aiming high. Against all odds he overcame every dream killer and assignment assassin that came against him.

Joseph achieved big because he dreamed big.

When life is over, you will never have the hope of becoming more than what you had the audacity to dream for, so if you're going to dream, dream big!

Precious dreamer with your precious dreams, your destiny is too great, your future too promising, and your purpose too mighty to fall victim to any dream killer. From today forward you are going to see with clarity the people and situations that long to kill your dreams. You'll learn how to avoid these dream killers and be assured that victory and purpose are on the horizon.

The very best of your life to come is locked up in your dreams, and your future starts today.

Let the journey begin!

Chapter 1

Dare to Dream Big

Now Israel loved Joseph more than all his children,
because he was the son of his old age. Also
he made him a tunic of many colors.
• *Genesis 37:3* •

I'M A DADDY'S BOY, EVEN THOUGH I HAVE TWENTY- AND fourteen-year-old daughters and a seven-year-old son. Although my father has been in heaven since 2005 and I'm a grown man, still today I'm a daddy's boy. Ironically I am writing these words the Saturday night just before Father's Day. And as I sit here preparing this book about dream killers, I can't help but think of the greatest dreamer I ever knew, my dad. I love him so much, and I miss him every day.

Life never dealt my dad an easy hand, but he always held mine. He never had much. He had to quit school in the eighth grade to help take care of his family. He pastored his first church when he was seventeen and preached the gospel for fifty-five years. I grew up living in church parsonages (some worse than others!) and watched my dad dream big wherever he was. No matter how tough things got at our churches, Dad was always dreaming of the next great thing that was about to happen in his ministry. He had the boldness to dream in the toughest of times. His dreams were contagious, and I started dreaming with him. And I've never stopped!

Never forget—dreams are contagious!

Joseph was a daddy's boy too. The Bible declares that Israel (Jacob) loved Joseph more than all of his children. Joseph was the eleventh son of Jacob and the first son of the love of his life, Rachel.

Joseph was special to his father. He knew it, and everyone in the family knew it. Jacob reiterated this fact by giving his favorite son a special coat—a coat of many colors. This coat signified to the rest of his brothers that Joseph had been singled out and that he was different. Those who have great dreams and great destinies locked up within them have to be prepared and willing at times to be singled out, and most assuredly to be different. A true God-inspired dream will require it to be so.

As a believer you have been singled out in this world, and like it or not, you are different. Your heavenly Father has not provided you with a coat of many colors but rather a coat of His precious anointing and His mighty presence. Because of that, you are different, and that difference challenges and presses you to dream for so much more than the status quo.

Big dreamers do things differently from others. To dare to dream *big* is the difference that makes impossibilities a reality. Basketball superstar Michael Jordan was cut from his high school basketball team. However, he didn't give up. His philosophy: "I play to win. The day I stop improving is the day I walk away from the game."[1] He didn't just have a dream. He committed to shooting three hundred baskets a day, and his dream became a reality.

You must have vision to see your potential and the faith to believe you can accomplish your dreams. God has designed you to dream big. Joseph tapped into the courage to conquer regardless of what others thought of him. He chose to embrace what God showed him. But what made the difference? Joseph embraced his dream not knowing the journey it would take to get to his destination. The person who never gets started is forever destined to lose.

God imparts the vision.

You dare to dream.

So dream *big.*

It's Not *Who* You Are but *Whose* You are

Believers who aren't dreaming big have lost sight of the fact that they have been singled out by their heavenly Father, and that alone causes them to be different. The thing that set Joseph apart was not so much the reality of *who* he was but rather *whose* he was. He was the child of Rachel, his father's sweetheart, born out of great love—and that made him special and unique. And what makes you special and unique is not who you are, but *whose* you are.

The prophet of old said it best when he declared:

> I have redeemed you; I have called you by your name;
> *you are Mine!*
> —Isaiah 43:1, emphasis added

You have not only been born but also born again—out of the great love of the Father. *"For God so loved the world"* (John 3:16, emphasis added). God doesn't just love you, He *so* loves you. He loves you with an emphatic and intense love.

One of the reasons Joseph dared to dream big was because of his knowledge and awareness of whose he was. Something about that pressing truth in his life enabled him to be a man of big dreams and great aspirations. As a child of Almighty God, when you come to a realization not so much of who you are, but more importantly of whose you are—everything changes. You will not be satisfied to dream some small insignificant ho-hum, humdrum dream. On the contrary, *you will dare to dream big.*

This boy was dreaming of the sun, moon, and stars. His dreams were literally out of this world! He was dreaming at another level, in another dimension—beyond what he was, who he was, and even where he was at that precise moment in his life. God wants to give you a dream that goes beyond your present mind-set, your present mentality, and even your present reality.

The challenge is to come to a place where you are actually willing to believe that a dream so seemingly awesome and incredible could actually be from God and for you. A God-inspired dream invites you out of your mediocre and mundane world and into His marvelous and magnificent world. The truth is, when God gives you a dream, expect it to be a big one! If you can obtain your dream in your own strength, there's a good chance it's your idea and not God's dream.

Even Joseph's name spoke volumes about who he was and the incredible destiny that rested on his life. The literal definition for the name Joseph is this: "Jehovah has added."[2] His name strongly implies that he was a gift from God. Every time his brothers or anyone else addressed him, they would have to call him by his name, "Jehovah has added." Do you think there may have been times when Joseph's brothers (in frustration and anger) said to him, "Who do you think you are, God's gift to this family?"

> If you can obtain your dream in your own strength, there's a good chance it's your idea and not God's dream.

To which Joseph may have replied, "Well, yes. Yes, I am." And by the end of the story, when they were in danger of starving to death because of a horrific and devastating famine, it became crystal clear that this mighty dreamer really was a gift to his family straight from Jehovah!

As a dreamer, you are God's gift to someone in your life. One of the most essential things you must realize and consider is how your dream will influence others. Joseph's dream was given *to* him only, but it was not *for* him only—something his brothers did not understand until years later. In fact, the dream was more about them than they realized.

Your dream goes beyond your world—it touches your future and can manifest its purpose in others who would otherwise miss a blessing. Your dream is the gift that keeps on giving. Stop dreaming, and you will alter the course of future events intended to bring hope and provision for generations to come. Start dreaming and expect a brighter, better future.

Imagine if Joseph would not have possessed the determination and intestinal fortitude to follow his dream through to a manifested reality. An entire nation would have paid the price. Generations of people would have never existed because his family would have perished in famine.

The nation of Israel lives today and the Redeemer of humanity was born because one man dared to dream big and then follow that dream through until it happened.

Armed with that revelation, you must answer some intense questions: Who's counting on you to dream big? Who will suffer if you fail to dream big and then fight to see it come to pass? Somebody somewhere is depending on you and your dream. Unless your big dream is fulfilled, all could be lost for them.

Think of great dreamers in history. What if Martin Luther King Jr. had failed to dream big? Where would our nation be as it relates to civil rights? What if Thomas Edison had not dreamed big? We might still be in the dark! And what about great Christian leaders of the past? Where would the church be without people like Martin Luther, John Wesley, Jonathan Edwards, Smith Wigglesworth, William J. Seymour, Aimee Semple McPherson, and so many others who had the courage to dream big concerning the things of God? What condition might the church be in without great dreamers?

In one way or another all of us have benefited because of someone else's big dream. In this "it's-all-about-me world" we live in today, we have mistakenly assumed that our dreams are for us and about us only. The reality, however, is quite the contrary.

Ultimately a true dream from the heart of God has a whole lot more to do with uplifting, blessing, and helping others. There is a real possibility that if your dreams bless you and only you, then God is not the source of your dreams! *God dreams* are the ones that when fulfilled they affect and influence others.

Big dreams entail big risks. Southwest Airlines cofounder Herb Kelleher was willing to risk his career for four years (and his own money) while he fought in the courtrooms to get Southwest Airlines off the ground.

> There is a real possibility that if your
> dreams bless you and only you, then God
> is not the source of your dreams!

Even though competing airlines battled against Southwest legally, Kelleher was willing to risk everything to "fight the good fight."[3] Why? Because he believed so strongly in the dream that nothing else mattered.

Pablo Picasso once said, "Everything you can imagine is real."[4] If everything you can imagine is real, and you can start the creation process simply by dreaming it, why not dream big?

Pay close attention to Joseph's situation. At the time he was under the most intense attack, he was dreaming for those who were not even dreaming for themselves! That's why when you dream, you need to *dream big*.

God may be giving you a dream for someone who cannot or will not dream for themselves! Those of you who have children really understand and comprehend this concept. Long before your children are mature enough to dream for themselves, you dream for them! You dream of their success, you dream of their happiness, you dream of their joy and their future. You dream of a victorious and productive tomorrow for them when they are not able to see anything past their today.

In reality, a dream that encompasses only self isn't that big of a dream. Those who dream only for themselves aren't really dreaming big. Dreams that are only self-serving and self-consumed are actually the smallest dreams of all. The biggest dreams, the best dreams, are the ones that wind up including, influencing, and blessing others.

As you'll see in the next chapter, dreams are very powerful. Today make up your mind that you won't waste your time dreaming for something small and insignificant. If you're going to dream—remember *whose* you are! And empowered with that knowledge and revelation, be like Joseph and *dare to dream big*!

Chapter 2

The Power of a Dream

And Pharaoh said to Joseph, "I have had a dream, and there
is no one who can interpret it. But I have heard it said of
you that you can understand a dream, to interpret it."
• *Genesis 41:15* •

ALBERT EINSTEIN, ABRAHAM LINCOLN, DR. MARTIN
Luther King Jr., Steve Jobs, Bill Gates, Walt Disney, and
Joseph: Can you guess what links these people together? They
were all prolific dreamers.

It is impossible to adequately describe the power of a dream.
When Walt Disney spoke of dreaming, he underscored this fact.
He said, "If you can dream it, you can do it. Always remember
that this whole thing was started with a dream and a mouse."[1]
The far-reaching influence of the Disney empire began with the
dream of one man. The Walt Disney Company earned almost
$43 billion last fiscal year.[2]

Dreams are powerful things.

Without dreams there would be no light bulbs, airplanes,
train tracks, or interstate systems. Imagine a life without tele-
phones, computers, indoor plumbing, or automobiles.

Big dreamers change the world and make it a better place. Don't underestimate the power of a dream—especially yours!

God can release a dream in your life so powerful that it will cause forward momentum to manifest like you never thought possible. Joseph had a dream that was so explosive it propelled him into supernatural promotion.

> God showed Joseph the promise of the dream but not the process. He was required to live out the process.

Recently, while rereading the story of Joseph in my Bible I was taken by something very interesting and powerful. Over significant portions of Scripture revolving around Joseph, there were subheadings describing what is about to occur in his life story. I want to share these with you as we begin to delve deeper into Joseph's life in this book. I believe they will help you discover the power of one man's dream, even when things seemed to be going wrong.

1. **Joseph dreams of greatness.** This was the first subheading in my Bible. Joseph had an amazing and profound dream of greatness. He was surely excited at this point and ready to see how this was going to pan out. It must have been a thrilling time!

2. **Joseph sold by his brothers.** The first subheading spoke of Joseph's great dream, the second of his horrific nightmare! Within the first twelve verses of Genesis chapter 37 Joseph had to contend with trouble. He was sold into bondage by his own flesh and blood.

3. **Joseph a slave in Egypt.** Joseph had dreamed of being a great ruler, yet in that moment he was a slave. He must have felt anything but great, and nothing like a ruler.

4. **The prisoners' dreams.** Joseph interpreted the dreams of prisoners only because he was in prison himself! Think about it: he had dreams of greatness, and now he was in prison after being falsely accused of attempted rape. Things didn't seem to be going along very well, huh? And you think you have trouble!

5. **Pharaoh's dreams.** Wait a minute; Joseph had these great and fantastic dreams, and he seemed to be in an unstoppable dilemma of frustration and failure. He was working on everyone's dream but his own.

6. **Joseph's rise to power.** After close to fifteen years of struggle, finally Joseph rises to power. His dream came to pass!

There are some very powerful lessons that can be gleaned from Joseph and his journey. God gave him incredible dreams, and then he went through an intense process. God showed Joseph the promise of the dream but not the process. He was required to live out the process. And so am I, and so are you.

The dream that God showed Joseph was so powerful that it survived even in the hardest of times. Look at Joseph's beginning. He started out in the land of Canaan, with his family. The word *Canaan* means lowland or low place. Before he ever rose to the high place of honor, recognition, and position, he had to endure the low place.

Everyone endures low places on the way to the fulfillment of their dreams. It's important to note that without the low places in life, there would be no high places. In the low places you gain strength; in the high places you gain perspective. Joseph rose to the high place of authority, but not before enduring the lowly (Canaan) places of life.

What's in a Name?

It is also worth noting that when Pharaoh promoted Joseph, he changed his name.

> And Pharaoh called Joseph's name Zaphnath-Paaneah. And he gave him as a wife Asenath, the daughter of Poti-Pherah priest of On. So Joseph went out over all the land of Egypt.
> —GENESIS 41:45

Pharaoh changed Joseph's name to Zaphnath-Paaneah. I know what you're thinking. Why didn't he just change his name to Bob? That would have been a whole lot easier name to deal with! But Pharaoh actually had a reason for changing Joseph's name to Zaphnath-Paaneah. When Pharaoh changed Joseph's name, he was describing who and what he believed Joseph was.

Joseph's new name gives incredible insight of who Joseph was in the eyes of those he influenced. *Strong's Concordance* defines Zaphnath-Paaneah as meaning "treasury of the glorious rest." It is very easy to understand why Joseph was given this name when you read the following passage of Scripture revolving around the time he interpreted Pharaoh's dreams.

> And Pharaoh said to Joseph, "I have had a dream, and there is no one who can interpret it. But I have heard it said of you that you can understand a dream, to interpret it." So Joseph answered Pharaoh, saying,

"It is not in me; God will give Pharaoh an answer of peace."

—GENESIS 41:15–16

Then Pharaoh related not one but two dreams to Joseph. Suddenly all eyes turned to Joseph to see if he understood the meaning of the dreams.

> Then Joseph said to Pharaoh, "The dreams of Pharaoh are one; God has shown Pharaoh what He is about to do.... Indeed seven years of great plenty will come throughout all the land of Egypt; but after them seven years of famine will arise, and all the plenty will be forgotten in the land of Egypt; and the famine will deplete the land. So the plenty will not be known in the land because of the famine following, for it will be very severe. And the dream was repeated to Pharaoh twice because the thing is established by God, and God will shortly bring it to pass. Now therefore, let Pharaoh select a discerning and wise man, and set him over the land of Egypt. Let Pharaoh do this, and let him appoint officers over the land, to collect one-fifth of the produce of the land of Egypt in the seven plentiful years. And let them gather all the food of those good years that are coming, and store up grain under the authority of Pharaoh, and let them keep food in the cities. Then that food shall be as a reserve for the land for the seven years of famine which shall be in the land of Egypt that the land may not perish during the famine."
>
> So the advice was good in the eyes of Pharaoh and in the eyes of all his servants.
>
> —GENESIS 41:25, 29–36

Joseph interpreted the dream of Pharaoh, and because of that Egypt survived a devastating famine. No wonder Pharaoh saw

Joseph as a glorious treasure. He saw him as someone who was to be valued and cherished. Can you imagine this? After spending years feeling worthless and of no value to his own family, Joseph is called a treasure by the most powerful man in the world.

You and your dream are valuable and precious. You must persevere in your pursuit because at the right time the right people will recognize that very fact! There was so much power in the dream of Joseph, that when it manifested, it produced glorious rest and favor. Now that's a dream worth having, a dream that produces glorious rest.

There is almost nothing worse that living life in continual strife and strivings. It is a formidable thing to rest in God. Even as you're reading this book, it is time to believe the Lord for a dream that will bring rest and peace to you and to those around you. It's time for you to have rest in your mind, rest in your ministry, rest in your family, and rest in finances. In fact, wherever you need rest, claim it now in Jesus's name!

It's Time for Life-Giving Dreams

Let's look a little deeper into this powerful name that Joseph was given. The Egyptian understanding of the name *Zaphnath-Paaneah* means "savior of the age."

There was so much power in the dream of Joseph that when it was fulfilled, the Egyptians saw him as the savior of the age. They perceived that without Joseph, and consequently his dream, they would have surely perished. We all know that God was the savior that age and is the savior of every age. But never forget, God used Joseph and his incredible dream!

Joseph and his precious dream were life-giving to those around him. The most powerful dreams are life-giving dreams. Your dream is a God-inspired dream when it promotes life in others.

From a Hebrew perspective Joseph's new name implied that

he was a "revealer of secrets." Joseph was incredibly gifted at interpreting the dreams of others, and this is without question. He interpreted the dreams of the baker and butler in prison, and then that of Pharaoh. He understood exactly what each of their dreams meant and what they implied.

> Your dream is a God-inspired dream
> when it promotes life in others.

That was amazing. It would have been a tragic thing, however, if he would have understood everybody else's dream but failed to comprehend his own.

Have you ever known folks who seemed to know what was the right course for everyone else, yet they were clueless when it came to their own? Great dreams are most powerful when they are fully comprehended by the person who is dreaming them. It is very important to dream with clarity. Foggy and unclear dreams create misty, unfocused lives.

Be clear about your dreams, about what it is you desire, and what it is you're in pursuit of. Clarity is a major step toward victory. A lack of clarity and clearness will produce a lack of precision as it relates to the pursuit of your dreams. Know what your dreams are, why you have them, and then get busy pursuing them.

Another reason that dreams are so powerful is because dreams are incredible hope replenishers. Where would you be in life during your most difficult times were it not for your ability to hold on to your dreams? Hope is released in your life when you keep a firm grip on your dreams.

Many of you are holding on to hope right this very moment. You are grasping your dream with all your heart. You may be hanging on to your dream about a ministry opportunity, a family issue, a career change, or anything else precious to you. As you look at your circumstances, sometimes it's hard to see how your God-given dreams will pan out and materialize.

But hang on; nothing releases hope like a dream.

A dream tells you that no matter what it looks like, it's not over. No matter what you're facing right now, it's not finished. Paul understood this and related the power of hope to the church in Rome, encouraging them to maintain hope during times of trouble and persecution.

> Rejoicing in hope, patient in tribulation, continuing steadfastly in prayer.
> —ROMANS 12:12

He said, "Rejoicing in hope!" There is great joy in hope. It's one thing to have joy when your dream is realized, but it's another thing to experience joy through the process.

Maintaining your dream creates an atmosphere of joy even when times are not joyful. One of the most effective dream killers is a joyless life. The enemy will do everything he can to rob you of every drop of joy in your existence. When he robs you of your joy, he effectively steals your hope.

When there is a famine of hope in your life, your dreams are often snuffed out. Decide right now to dream with hope and to dream joyfully. Be optimistic and expect the best!

I heard a story one time about an experiment conducted on two little boys—one an optimist, the other a pessimist. The little pessimistic boy was given a pony, and all he could find to say were negative words: "This pony isn't really mine. Somebody is going to take this pony from me. I can't feed this pony. This pony is too tall for me to ride anyway." Negative statement after negative statement came out of his depressed little mouth. Even though he had always wanted a pony, he was filled with negativity.

The little optimistic boy wasn't given a pony but a room

completely filled with horse dung. He jumped in that room and started wading right through it all as if he was looking for something. He was laughing, hooping, hollering, and yelling. One of the scientists seemed shocked and asked him, "Why in the world are you so happy?"

To which the little boy replied, "With all this dung, there has got to be a horse in here somewhere!"

Hang on to your dream, and do it with joy! Nobody likes a grouchy dreamer.

The Journey Changes You, Not Your Dream

The next thing to note is this: Joseph's dream never changed. Exactly what God showed Joseph is exactly what came to pass. Joseph never watered down his dreams or made concessions or compromises because of his circumstances. When God gives you a dream, expect it to come to pass *fully*.

> The journey never changed Joseph's *dream*; the journey changed *Joseph*.

Even though the process to the fulfillment of his dreams was more intense than anything Joseph could have imagined, the journey never changed his dream. No matter how hard times were or how intense conditions got in Joseph's life, his dream remained steadfast and unchanging.

The journey never changed Joseph's *dream*; the journey changed *Joseph*.

That's one of the greatest powers a God-given dream has. The process to its fulfillment does more than transform your circumstances; it transforms you.

One of the strengths that Joseph possessed because of his

great dreams was this: no matter how tough things got, he knew things would get better. His dreams were always a beacon of light and hope during the stormy times. He was able to remind himself, "This is not the fulfillment of the dream," so he knew he had to keep going.

Your great dreams will give you the strength to keep on going. If you're not where you know your dream said you would be, don't stop; keep going. Don't go on the strength of what you see; go on the strength of what your dream said and what it showed you. Never underestimate the power of a dream!

Now is not the time to settle, to compromise, or to give up. Now is the time to be tenacious and resolute concerning your dream.

Just look at Joseph, and chances are, you can probably see yourself. Long before Joseph was ever honored with the name Zaphnath-Paaneah, he endured many low places. Before he was viewed as a treasure and honored as a secret revealer, he was hated, scorned, discarded, and marginalized. Before he ever sat on a throne, he sat alone.

He started out in a low place called Canaan. There he was despised and rejected by his family. That's pretty low. But then he goes lower, into the pit. Then he goes even lower as he is sold into slavery. It certainly doesn't seem like things could ever get lower than that, but they did. He is falsely accused of attempted rape and thrown in prison.

And when it seemed he had reached the bottom, he helped the butler of the king interpret his dream. He was promised by this butler that he would be remembered before Pharaoh. But for two long years he languished behind lowly prison bars. Yet through it all, through Joseph's lowest times, his powerful dreams gave him strength.

Whatever you are facing, never underestimate the power of your dream! The dream God has placed inside of you is able to give you the strength and intestinal fortitude to press forward regardless of what you might be seeing right now.

You may not be where you want to be, but in Jesus's name don't allow that to kill your dream. Your dream is alive and well because you are alive and well.

You're about to learn about dream killers in the next chapter, but never forget: the dream God has placed within you is greater than anything that is going on without. It's not too late to claim every part of your dream. C. S. Lewis said, "You are never too old to set another goal or to dream a new dream."[3] Never make the mistake of underestimating the power of a dream.

Chapter 3

Understanding a
Dream Killer

And they hated him yet the more
for his dreams, and for his words.
• *Genesis 37:8, KJV* •

ATE IS A STRONG WORD. IT EXPRESSES AN EMOTIONAL attitude toward people and things that are opposed, detested, and despised. You use it when you are describing someone whom you wish to have no contact or relationship with. It is the opposite of love. Love draws and unites; hate separates and divides. To be hated is to be considered a foe or an enemy—utterly unappealing.

To be hated by your enemy or archrival is one thing, but to be hated by your family is another. This was the predicament of Joseph's relationship with his brothers. It is a terrible thing to be hated for your dreams. Joseph lived under the ongoing pressure of that disturbing, crushing, and cruel reality in his life.

He was hated for his dreams. Can you imagine? I can think of few things worse than having great God-given, God-designed, God-ordained dreams and then being despised for them. Joseph's brothers not only hated his dreams, but they also hated him for dreaming them. He dreamed, and the fact that he dreamed caused him to be hated!

In their minds it was bad enough that he was a dreamer, but what really brought his brothers' anger and disgust to another level was that he had the audacity and the unmitigated gall to articulate his dreams. These *dream killers* seethed and boiled with hot fiery anger every time Joseph spoke up about his dreams.

This is a powerful lesson; there are those who will tolerate you as long as you keep your dreams to yourself, but as soon as you talk about your dreams, as soon as you put your dreams out there in the open, all of a sudden things begin to change. Their whole attitude and disposition toward you can be radically altered.

The real question is why. Why is it that there are those who hate and despise dreamers? An even more thought-provoking question is this: How does someone become a dream killer? Here are three answers to that question.

1. Dream killers become consumed by jealousy.

The number one concept that must be considered is the concept of jealousy. "But while his brothers were jealous of Joseph, his father wondered what the dreams meant" (Gen. 37:11, NLT).

Why were they jealous? Primarily for this reason: favor—he had the favor of the father in his life.

> Jacob loved Joseph more than any of his other children because Joseph had been born to him in his old age. So one day Jacob had a special gift made for Joseph—a beautiful robe. But his brothers hated Joseph because their father loved him more than the rest of them.
> —GENESIS 37:3–4, NLT

This is very significant. As a dreamer you must never be surprised when someone despises you because of the Father's favor in your life.

True dreamers, the ones who dream outside of their own ability and beyond the limits of their own natural potential, are dreamers who must have the favor of the heavenly Father in and over their lives.

> When you have a God-designed dream, it will only come to pass through His favor and faithfulness.

The heavenly Father will birth dreams within you that require His favor in order for them to manifest and materialize. His favor is the key. Without the favor of the heavenly Father, the dreams He has given you will never be attained. The reality is, God designed your dream to depend on Him!

When you have a God-designed dream, it will only come to pass through His favor and faithfulness. God will give you a dream, but then He will make sure the only way it will come true is through Him. Therefore, when it manifests, He gets all the glory! Plain and simple, you need God. And like it or not, there are times when God's favor in your life will breed contempt and hatred from others.

2. Dream killers feel threatened.

Dream killers are dealing with the disturbing reality that somehow someone else's great dream throws light on a deficiency in them, a character flaw in them, a lack of drive and determination in them.

So they are actually threatened by the dreamer. And it is out of that mind-set and mentality that they begin to act and react. Someone who feels threatened is hostile, hateful, mean, and nasty.

23

When Joseph shared his dream, his brothers felt threatened when he insinuated that he would be superior over them and that they would submit to his authority. His brothers responded and spoke out of their insecurities and lack of self-worth.

Most dream killers, no matter how confident they may seem on the outside, are actually wrestling and grappling with their own feelings of inadequacy on the inside. It is from that place of deep pain, from that place of frustration that they begin to lash out!

More often than not dream killers are people who are filled with and fueled by great and intense pain. It is impossible to understand them without first attempting to understand their pain. Let's look at the reaction of Joseph's brothers to try and gain a better understanding.

> His brothers responded, "So you think you will be our king, do you? Do you actually think you will reign over us?"
> —GENESIS 37:8, NLT

Virtually every time Joseph's brothers laid eyes on him, they felt pain. They felt the pain of being less than him, the pain of not measuring up to him, the pain of feeling inferior to him.

In order to ease their own pain, they began to plot and ploy the literal devastation and death not only of the dream but also, shamefully, the dreamer. Dominated and derailed by pain and frustration, jealousy and envy, they became assignment assassins and dream killers.

Remember now, his brothers *hated* him for his dreams and for his words. In the original language of the Old Testament this is extremely intense and strong. The word *hated* here in the Book of Genesis is the Hebrew word *sane*. The original translation means "to hate and to be hateful!" It is literally "hatred in action."

Their hatred was put on display each and every day. The Bible says that his brothers *"couldn't say a kind word to him"* (Gen. 37:4, NLT, emphasis added). They took every opportunity to be cruel, and they thoroughly and completely despised him. His everyday misery became their everyday policy. They were so threatened by him that they grew to hate him. This leads to our third answer.

3. Dream killers despise great destiny.

Joseph's brothers didn't feel their strongest hatred for his dreams, his words, or the obvious favoritism their father showed to him. Their most intense hatred was not even reserved for Joseph himself. What they hated most was his destiny! Why? Why in the world did they despise his destiny so much?

The answer is surprisingly simple: *they perceived that his destiny was greater than theirs!* They recognized something about him he may not have ever recognized in himself at that time.

It was obvious to them that something was different about Joseph. After all, he was not required to tend to the sheep, work in the fields, or spend long days in the hot sun.

> Soon after this, Joseph's brothers went to pasture their father's flocks at Shechem. When they had been gone for some time, Jacob said to Joseph, "Your brothers are pasturing the sheep at Shechem. Get ready, and I will send you to them."
> —GENESIS 37:12–13, NLT

To them Joseph was a daddy's boy. He was the chosen one. After all, his fingernails were never dirty. He didn't break a sweat, carry a load, or work a day in his life. No, he got to hang around Dad. They probably felt he was treated like royalty. He was reserved to accomplish Dad's wish list, like run errands and deliver messages for his father.

They saw "the handwriting on the wall." Joseph was being

groomed to be something extraordinary, and extraordinary often intimidates ordinary.

They despised Joseph's destiny because deep down inside their own hearts they knew his dreams could actually be fulfilled. Why else would they feel so threatened by him, so threatened they were willing to kill him? Their own insecurity caused them to declare war on his destiny. It can be a terrifying season in your life when someone declares war on your destiny.

At times you may have to endure the great and intense attack of dream killers. But that attack proves something very powerful: *your dream killers believe in you.*

Dream killers only fight whom and what they believe in! Those who may be fighting you the hardest and resisting you the most are only doing so because—whether they realize it or not—they believe in you! Let that revelation sink in. Your most intense attacks come from those who believe in you! Even if they say you can't, their actions prove that deep down they really think you can!

> **You may have to endure the attack of dream killers. But that attack proves something very powerful: *your dream killers believe in you.***

In a strange way, then, you can take comfort and encouragement from the presence of a dream killer. Because the presence of a dream killer can actually be a sign that you're on the right track and the best is yet to come! When you have great destiny, the enemy will always send dream killers to try to disrupt, delay, and even destroy that destiny.

Joseph was hated, and the hatred Joseph endured was so much more than just a superficial nonaggressive kind of hatred that exists just under the surface. Hatred like that is disguised by sarcastic smiles and smirks. These kinds of haters are the most common and hate undercover. They lack the intestinal fortitude or just plain guts to express outwardly what beats so strongly in their hearts. These people are the ones who act as if they want to eat you up to your face and do eat you up behind your back!

Joseph, however, dealt with a much more savage kind of hatred—a hatred that was totally unhidden, up close and personal. Joseph had to contend with a hatred that was right out in the open. And this hatred was from none other than his own family.

What's a Dreamer to Do?

Ironically, and often times painfully, the enemy will use those closest to you to try to destroy your dreams. When I say he uses those closest to you, I don't mean close in proximity; I mean close in relationship, people you have heart ties with. Someone who should *have* your back becomes the one who *stabs* you in the back.

This is the source of perhaps the greatest pain of all: when the people you love the most hate you for your dreams the most. What a quandary it is when the dreamer is faced with some of these heart-wrenching questions.

- What do I do when I love my dream killer?

- Do I choose my dream, or do I choose my dream killer?

- Do I abandon my God-given dream, or do I abandon my dream killer, even though I may love them?

- What price am I willing to pay for my dream? What if my dream costs me everything?

Not everyone is going to be happy with your dreams! As I've shared in this chapter, dream killers possess three basic qualities: they are jealous, they feel threatened, and they despise anyone's destiny they feel is greater than theirs.

So what are you to do when you are faced by dream killers? Here are seven keys to help you hold on to your dreams until you fulfill your destiny.

1. *Be alert.* Even those who pose as your friends, such as coworkers, and yes, even your family members may turn against you when you begin to dream. Like a snake in the grass they may strike at any time, ready to unleash venom that could potentially expose the dream killer in them.

2. *Expect opposition.* Don't be taken by surprise! Ask God for discernment on a regular basis, and then trust it when He gives it. Press through! Follow through on your dream, and don't stop just to pacify others.

3. *Protect your dreams.* Step away from relationships when you suspect a person is a dream killer. Feeding your dream may mean starving a negative relationship. Once you realize someone is a dream killer, keep a distance, limit their access to your life, and never let them influence your decisions.

4. *Nourish right relationships.* Surround yourself with like-minded individuals who will support your dream and never kill it.

5. *Stay on course.* Many times people forsake their dreams because they struggle to break away from unhealthy relationships. Once you've decided that

holding on to your dreams will require you to let some people go, whatever the cost you must stay on course.

6. *Pursue with passion.* Go ahead and keep chasing your dream, even if others disapprove. Your dream is your destiny, and destiny requires pursuit.

7. *Press through the pain.* Pain is often the price tag. Realize you will not please everyone when you pursue your dream. Opposition is painful, but not as painful as falling short of your potential. And even if you have to endure pain because of your dream, press through the pain and into the promise.

The fulfillment of Joseph's dream cost him everything—everything he knew and, for a season, everyone he knew. However, it becomes crystal clear as you study the life of Joseph that on some level he finally understood his dream killers. He must have, in some significant way, comprehended their pain. Because of that he never allowed himself to be dominated and controlled by bitterness.

The moment you become overwhelmed by bitterness, the slow and painful death of your dreams begins.

The concept of mental bitterness comes from the idea of something that has a sharp or unpleasant taste. You speak of something being bitter if it causes grief or is hard to bear: "a bitter defeat," "bitter failure." You also speak of a "bitter loss" when someone's death has caused great grief.

When you allow bitterness to enter into the equation, you lose every time. Bitterness is neither consistent nor rational. A bitter person is his own worst enemy. It is very difficult to maintain any kind of relationship with a chronically bitter person, and bitterness is a major contributing cause of marital and family problems.

The moment you become overwhelmed by bitterness, the slow and painful death of your dreams begins. It is obvious that Joseph loved his family, and he somehow lived above bitterness and rose above his dream killers, because in the end his dream provided a place for them all.

In the next chapter you'll learn about turning obstacles into opportunities. Start by letting go of the obstacle of bitterness. Be honest with God, and confess any resentment, bitterness, or unforgiveness you've been harboring in your heart. He knows how hard it can be to let go, but He also knows the tremendous blessings awaiting you when you do!

Chapter 4

Dream Your Way Out

Now Joseph had a dream....
Then he dreamed still another dream.
• *Genesis 37:5, 9* •

As we study the life of Joseph, there is absolutely no questioning the fact that he grew up in an extremely harsh, tension-filled environment. But what you must get ahold of is this: in the midst of all the negativity, in the midst of all the pain and turmoil, right in the middle of incredible resistance and friction—God gave him a dream.

The thing I find so awesome about God is His ability to transform obstacles into opportunities. God uses everything—even your difficulties—in the great recipe of life to develop your destiny. Your worst and most painful times can become tools in His hands to birth great things in your life. Your most disastrous and heart-wrenching moments can actually become tremendous seasons of *dream development*.

Perhaps the most pressing reality to consider in the life of Joseph is that in an atmosphere of misery, negativity, and pressure, something very powerful and significant happened: Joseph became hungry to dream. He so desperately wanted transition and transformation in his life that he began to dream of it. The meanness of the moment and cruelness that he was forced to endure was actually what God used to awaken all the mighty dreams within him.

> The thing I find so awesome about God is His ability to transform obstacles into opportunities.

What he perceived as antagonism, God perceived as an alarm clock—because nothing wakes up the dreamer like *trouble*. Had Joseph not been forced to grapple with all he had to grapple with, to live with all he had to live with, he would have probably never begun to dream. He would have been soothed by the satisfaction of his situation. Instead he was pressured by the perplexity of his problems.

Comprehending this alarms and amazes me at the same time. God placed Joseph in a situation where he would literally be required to dream his way out. Trouble is what caused him to dream! *God uses trouble.*

This is an amazing revelation: God trusted Joseph with trouble. He knew trouble would not make Joseph quit; trouble would make him dream. What about you? Can God trust you with trouble?

Will you quit or dream when the going gets tough? Some of you may be going through trouble right now. Don't quit! Dream! Be encouraged even in your trouble. God is trusting you with that trouble because it's time to dream.

No one can deny that Joseph was in a great predicament, but his destiny was greater than his dilemma! However, his dilemma became the catalyst for his dream. His dissatisfaction over his circumstances required him to dream his way out.

Plainly stated, this boy's pain is what caused him to dream! I believe Joseph started dreaming of a brighter day, a day when he would be loved, respected, and esteemed by his brothers. Joseph began to dream of a greater existence and a better life. In an atmosphere of pain, he dreamed of peace. In a reality of binding boundaries, he dreamed of boundless blessings. In trouble, he dreamed of triumph. But you cannot ignore or lose sight of the fact that it was the dilemma that developed the dreamer.

Like Father, Like Son

The Bible does not tell us if Joseph's father, Jacob, ever told his sons about his past—the dilemma of deception with his father, Isaac, to gain the birthright, the struggles he had with his twin brother, Esau, or the life-changing dream he himself had. (See Genesis 28.) But I find it interesting that Joseph was a dreamer just like his daddy. As far as I know, he was the only son who inherited his father's passion to dream. Joseph had his share of drama due to family strife and the misunderstanding of his purpose within God's plan. But so did his dad.

Jacob was the son of Isaac and the grandson of Abraham. This family was selected by God to be the foundation of faith and the origin of the Hebrew nation. Before Jacob was born, God had determined that there was something special about him and that he would be the one who would carry the family lineage to promise. His mother was barren—cursed in their culture—doomed and unable to bare children. But Isaac prayed to the Lord on behalf of his wife, believing that she would conceive. And God answered his request. She conceived.

During her pregnancy Rebekah felt a struggle inside her—a wrestling match between the twins in her womb. It troubled her to the point that she cried out to the Lord, trying to understand the meaning of her discomfort (Gen. 25:22). The Lord answered her with a prophetic word concerning the destiny of her children.

> Two nations are in your womb, two people shall
> be separated from your body; one people shall be
> stronger than the other, and the older shall serve the
> younger.
>
> —GENESIS 25:23

When the twins were born, Esau (meaning, "hairy") was the first to come out, and then his brother, Jacob (meaning, "heel catcher" or "to grasp the heel"), had a grip on Esau's ankle. This seemed meaningless at the time, but it illustrates the impending struggles these brothers would endure, and it demonstrated Jacob's future.

What would make an infant grasp his brother's heel? What did this action portray? Jacob was too young to understand the significance of his future, so his action was divinely inspired by a prophetic word the Lord had given his mother, *"And the older shall serve the younger."* Even at birth Jacob was grabbing for the dream inside him.

Years later, impatient to receive the promise, Rebekah decided to fulfill this prophecy. Despite Jacob's hesitancy and concern, her plan to trick her husband to bless him would label Jacob as a "deceiver" in the eyes of his father. But she convinced Jacob to go along and to allow the consequences to be her trouble and not his (Gen. 27:12–13).

The deception would create a mountain of strife and struggle in the family. Concerned about retaliation from Esau, Jacob lived in hiding for years. It is in this context that Jacob, at the end of his rope and running for his life, had a dream that changed everything. Despite his actions, God had a plan. Through Jacob He would fulfill his covenant with Abraham (Gen. 28:13–14).

In his hour of desperation and despair Jacob dreamed a dream.

> Then he dreamed, and behold, a ladder was set up on
> the earth, and its top reached to heaven; and there the
> angels of God were ascending and descending on it.
> —GENESIS 28:12

When it looked like family, friends, and favor had abandoned him, he dreamed his way out! The Lord reassured Jacob that regardless of what had happened up to that point, God had his back. The Bible says he left *Beersheba*, which means "well of oath (favor)" or "place of good fortune and favor," and went toward Haran (v. 10). *Haran* means "road, route, or caravan." Jacob left the "place of favor" and was in "route" on a journey, but he did not know his destination. He did not know where to go.

In his hour of desperation, when it looked like favor was left behind, he traveled down a path—a road that looked like a dead end, and then he dreamed a dream. When he woke up, he was in shock. Puzzled by his dream, he recognized that the place where he had been sleeping was not what it seemed.

> Then Jacob awoke from his sleep and said, "Surely the
> LORD is in this place, and I did not know it." And he
> was afraid and said, "How awesome is the place! This
> is none other than the house of God, and this is the
> gate of heaven!"
> —GENESIS 28:16–17

Jacob was in a hard place but declared, *"Surely the Lord is in this place, and I did not know it!"* God is in your hardest places, even when you don't know it! How many times has God been with you and you were not aware? Even now, even if everything seems to be in crisis, be encouraged! God is with you.

Jacob found himself at the end of his rope—helpless and hopeless—but his place of obscurity became his place of opportunity. His dream revealed that he had an open gate to heaven, so he named the place *Bethel*, "the house of God." God shows up at unlikely times in unlikely places.

Jacob's long, lonely road suddenly became a highway to heaven. In the middle of his darkest hour he dreamed of an open heaven, a place of light. Hope dawned on a new day.

When circumstances, disappointment, and despair surround you, there's light at the end of the tunnel. What appears to be a road to destruction can become your road to destiny when you dream your way out!

As I said earlier, Joseph inherited his ability to dream from his father, Jacob. Joseph was also the fulfillment of Jacob's dream. Joseph had a deposit inside of him from his father's journey to destiny, and that deposit was the catalyst for fulfilling his own destiny.

Many times your dreams are fulfilled in your children. What my dad dreamed to accomplish in his lifetime is being fulfilled in and though me today. It was his desires, his efforts, and his accomplishments that paved the way for me to become a dreamer. He dreamed of a great ministry and passed that spirit of a dreamer to me. In Jesus's name I will pass it to my children.

Don't Wait for a Clear Path

Jacob dreamed his way out before the road become clear. That's how you do it. You dream before the road is clear. You dream before you know which way to turn. You dream before you know where you're headed. You dream your way out!

When my wife and I first became pastors of our church, Calvary Christian Center, it was an extremely difficult situation. The facilities were in disrepair, and we had a small and dwindling congregation, horrific debt, and financial problems. It was so intense that we didn't even know if we would have lights or electricity for many of the church services. Our congregation was mostly senior adults, and these precious people were holding on with all their might.

Prior to coming to Calvary, God had graced our lives with a successful evangelistic ministry. Needless to say, we were happy and had no financial worries whatsoever. The last thing we wanted to do was pastor any church, but most especially a struggling one. But in God's sovereign plan and through an incredible series of events we wound up pastoring this church.

The pressure we were under is almost indescribable. There were those who doubted our church and thought it could never do anything significant in our area. Truthfully, because of past problems, there were those who even despised our church in the community. It was tough, to say the least.

We had limited staff and no money. In fact, we owed money all over town! We were constantly denied credit at local stores; our school was losing multiplied thousands and thousands of dollars a month. It seemed there was no light at the end of the tunnel. We were in an impossible situation in the natural realm. However, our dilemma birthed our desperation. And in that desperation we began to dream *big*!

We literally began to dream of everything we did not have at that time. We began dreaming of something we believed our church could become—a thriving, multicultural, multiracial, multidenominational, worldwide outreach center that would minister to the masses. We dreamed of a day when thousands would attend our church and millions would experience our message through radio, television, and the Internet.

We dreamed of ministries to the homeless, which would be supremely and intensely dedicated to the least, the last, and the lost. We dreamed of sidewalk Sunday school, prison outreach, and helping and loving at-risk and underprivileged kids in our communities. We dreamed of a place filled with so much of the love of Jesus that anyone and everyone could come and connect—people from every race, every conceivable educational and financial background, from every place and position in life.

We dreamed of world-class ministries to children, teens, and young adults. We dreamed of an educationally excellent and spiritually nurturing school and children's center, as well as a kingdom-training, warrior-raising school of ministry.

> If you are contending with tremendous trouble, God might be using that trouble—not to destroy your dream, but to develop it.

We dreamed of state-of-the-art facilities and counseling offices for those struggling with family issues and personal problems. We dreamed of a church where the atmosphere was incredible and awesome—a place that was all held together by God's mighty power and love! And the God who gave us the dream has made it all come to pass and so much more! However, the fact is, it was our trouble that caused us to dream. It was the desperation of our dilemma that awakened the dreamer within us.

We all go through times in our lives when we endure seemingly senseless seasons of attack, pain, and frustration. But in these hard times you need to obtain a "God's-eye" view of your circumstances. Could it be the very thing you're facing right now is what God desires to use to awaken and unlock the great dreams He has placed within you? If you are contending with tremendous trouble, God might be using that trouble—not to destroy your dream, but to develop it.

What if you're encountering that situation at this very moment because it is time for you to dream your way out of your problem and into His plan? You may be in an intense place right now, a place where nothing seems to be going the way you planned, a place where you are enduring life in many ways rather than enjoying it. In this season you might be contending with problems, people, and persecution. It might be a place where you are uncomfortable and unfulfilled, a place where nothing seems to make sense. But hear this word: *dream your way out!*

Joseph never got out until he dreamed his way out—and neither will you!

- Dream your way out!

- Dream your way out of your mess and into your miracle!

- Dream your way out of your problem and into God's promise!

- Dream your way out of your desperate dilemma and into your divine destiny!

The enemy is trying to use the issues of your life to kill, steal, and destroy your divine destiny. But with God the opposite is true. He will use your stresses, your strains, your struggles, and even your strife to awaken the dreamer in you!

Even if things are tough right now, it's not time to quit in fear and frustration. The trouble is not going to *shake* you; it's going to *make* you! You're about to discover that "the pit ain't it!" Now is not the time to wave the white flag of surrender in the face of adversity. On the contrary, it's time to dream your way out!

Chapter 5

The Pit Ain't It

Then they took him and cast him into a pit. And
the pit was empty; there was no water in it.
• *Genesis 37:24* •

W E HAVE ALL HAD SEASONS IN OUR LIVES WHEN WE HAVE had certain goals, destinations, and dreams in mind, only to be jarred by the fact that where we thought we were headed is not where we actually end up. The good news is, God has a plan. The bad news is, sometimes it doesn't seem like it! One of the greatest illustrations of this is exposed as we study the life of Joseph. He dreamed of the palace, but he found himself in the pit!

Don't kid yourself; Joseph must have had some serious questions while he was in that pit. Hard questions always arise when your dream and your reality are in contradiction to each other. It must have been a sobering moment when Joseph came to terms with the painful truth of his situation.

Surely he pondered within himself, "Why am I here?" He must have thought, "I can't believe I let myself get into this mess.

When will I ever learn? How could I have trusted these jokers? Look where it got me."

Joseph had been asked by his father to go and check on his brothers, and he jumped at the chance. He was actually being kind, and look where it got him. His kindness landed him in the pit, and who had placed him there? The people he was being kind to; those he had been sent to help were the ones who had thrown him in the pit.

There will be times in your life when in route to your destiny you'll encounter people you love, and you assume by association that they will love you in return. But no matter how hard you try, you will never make everyone happy. What do you do when the very people you trust turn against you? What do you do when you are wronged, even when you are doing everything right?

The question demands an answer, "How can bad things happen when I'm trying to be so good?" If you live long enough, you will face this dilemma many times. Just because it's God's will doesn't mean it will always be easy for you, or you will always be loved or celebrated.

The Bible says, "If you are reproached for the name of Christ, blessed are you, for the Spirit of glory and of God rests upon you" (1 Pet. 4:14). The word *reproached* can be better understood or reworded as "undeserved attack."

In other words, when you suffer an undeserved attack—and you will—the Spirit of glory and of God will rest upon you. Why? Because when you endure an undeserved attack, you are emulating Jesus.

When you are pushed into a pit, God will give you rest and times of refreshing, and He will instill hope inside of you. Even in the pit God will give you an expectation of release. Peter said, "The Spirit and the glory of God rest upon you." That's so awesome, because you can survive anything as long as His Spirit and His glory rest on you!

Notice, Peter said *God* will give you rest, not *people*. In the pit don't expect others to come running to your rescue. In fact, in the case of Joseph, his brothers sat down and ate while he was in the pit. They were enjoying a party while he was enduring the pit! They were not concerned about him.

You cannot afford to be codependent or to rely on others to get you out of the pit. Like it or not, very often, when others see you in your pit, they are more likely to leave you there than to make the effort to get you out.

They will stumble across your pit, look down into your dungeon of despair, and depending upon their viewpoint, will have a comment as to how or why you got yourself in the situation you are in. If this were a parable, it would sound something like this: A man fell into a pit and couldn't get out. Then one by one a group of people came by and gave their opinion of the pit experience.

- The subjective person said, "I feel for you in the pit."

- The objective person said, "It's logical that someone would fall into that pit."

- The Christian Scientist said, "You only think you're in a pit."

- The Pharisee said, "Only bad people fall into a pit."

- The mathematician said, "Have you calculated how you fell into that pit?"

- The news reporter said, "Can I do an exclusive story on you and your experience in the pit?"

- The fundamentalist said, "You must define your pit."

- The Calvinist said, "If you were saved, you wouldn't have fallen into that pit."

- The Wesleyan said, "You were saved until you fell into that pit."

- The Word of Faith person said, "Just confess it, brother: 'I'm not in a pit.'"

- The realist said, "Now that's what I call a pit."

- The geologist said, "I appreciate the rocks in your pit."

- The IRS agents said, "Have you paid taxes on this pit?"

- The county inspector said, "Do you have a permit for this pit?"

- The evasive person avoided the pit all together.

- The self-pitying person said, "You haven't seen anything until you've seen my pit!"

- The optimist said, "Things could be worse."

- The pessimist said, "Things will get worse."

But Jesus, seeing the man in the pit, reached down and began to lift him up and said, "Don't let the pit cause you to lose focus. I'll get you out one way or another. This is not where you belong." Plainly stated, *the pit ain't it!*

Destiny vs. Destination

It can be a confusing and frustrating time when you have palace dreams and pit realities. What in the world do you do when this painful scenario is being played out in your life? It is then that you must truly grasp the timing of the Lord. With God, timing is everything. The temptation you face is to judge your situation prematurely, to assume that where you're at is where you are destined to stay. You confuse destiny with destination.

> Then he said to him, "Please go and see if it is well with your brothers and well with the flocks, and bring back word to me." So he sent him out of the Valley of Hebron, and he went to Shechem.
> —Genesis 37:14

> And the man said, "They have departed from here, for I heard them say, 'Let us go to Dothan.'" So Joseph went after his brothers and found them in Dothan.
> —Genesis 37:17

> Then they took him and cast him into a pit. And the pit was empty; there was no water in it.
> —Genesis 37:24

In just ten verses look at how things changed.

> **The pit is just a portion and a part of the process;**
> **the process is what will lead you to the promise.**

Destination: what is it? It is a place of final purpose, but destiny often requires rough roads to get there. Joseph had to ask himself, "How did I end up here when I was headed for there?" Have you ever asked yourself that question? Joseph went to

Shechem, and from there he went to Dothan, but he ended up in a pit.

Joseph was sent by his father to locate his brothers. His journey was over eight miles to *Shechem,* which means "the portion back in the morning." Its significance in Israel's history was that it was "the high place." *Dothan* was another ten miles or more from Shechem, and it means "the place of two wells, the place of refreshing."

Joseph set out for Shechem, but his brothers were not there. He headed for the high place but didn't find what he was looking for, so he moved forward. Then at Dothan (the place of refreshing) he thought it would be a great place to be, but it didn't turn out that way. He ended up in the pit.

How did Joseph end up *here* when he was headed for *there*? Like Joseph, how many times have you been on a journey, seeking to get *there* but you ended up *here*? You were headed for a *high* place and wound up in a *dry* place. You anticipated a palace, but instead you landed in a pit.

Maybe you're in the pit right now. You started out looking for answers, so you strove to get to the high place, the place where God is. You were seeking for a refreshing in your marriage, ministry, career, family, or relationships. And then you discovered you're in a pit and said, "Lord, how did I get here?"

The well of refreshing is empty, void, lifeless, and without water; it's a dry season, a pit. You head for the high place and wind up in the dry place. Throughout your life your destiny will require you to endure many twist and turns, up and downs, and highs and lows. But when you find yourself in the pit, you must never forget: this is just a portion of your destiny; this is not your destination. If you are not careful, you will accept the pit as permanent, but the pit is not the end of your story!

One important coping mechanism when you find yourself in a pit is to remind yourself that you are on a journey and that where you are is just part of that journey. Empowered by that revelation, you must recognize and realize that the pit—no matter how dark and dim your current situation may be—is not the end! Your story is still being told; your story is not over.

Even if someone you love is in a rough, hard, and tough place right now, don't give up on them. Their story is not over, and neither is yours! The pit is just a portion and part of the process; the process is what will lead you to the promise.

> There are no shortcuts to divine destiny. Those who are looking for a shortcut will wind up being cut short!

The fact is, God often reveals to you a prophetic preview of the promise while not completely showing you the process. He knows that for most of you, if He allowed you to view the process, it might be too much for you. Seeing the process, you might give up prematurely rather than enduring the process until the promise is realized.

Anyone who has endured to any significant breakthrough in their lives knows there are no shortcuts to divine destiny. Those who are looking for a shortcut will wind up being cut short! You must progress through the process in its entirety; then and only then will the promise come into fruition.

No one is exempt from the process. It doesn't matter how gifted, talented, connected, or articulate you are; the pathway to the promise requires the process. God not only allows the process, but He also requires it. There are things you are destined to learn, know, and embrace that only the journey through God's predesigned process can teach you.

Power in the Pit

And they said one to another, Behold, this dreamer cometh. Come now therefore, and let us slay him, and cast him into some pit, and we will say, Some evil beast hath devoured him: and we shall see what will become of his dreams.

—GENESIS 37:19–20, KJV

This mighty man Joseph is proof that God will allow you to experience pit places of life. The question is, why? Why would a God who has already revealed the promise require the pit? Why not just allow you to bypass the pit and get on the fast track to the promise? Doesn't that sound great? There are two very important reasons why you cannot bypass the pit.

1. The Lord wants to reveal some new things to you about yourself.

God knows exactly and precisely what He has placed within you. Like it or not, there are things within you that will never manifest without some time in the pit. In His infinite wisdom God knows it's only the trial, heat, and adversity of the pit that will bring out much of what is hidden in you.

So the pit is not a place of death but discovery, for in the pit is where you see yourself! God will use the pit to show you who you really are and what you're truly made of. It's the pain, persecution, and predicament of the pit that produce the purest picture of you to you!

If you really want to discover who you are and what you're made of, get ready to spend some time in the pit! In the pit you realize that you are a survivor; you recognize that even though you may be in trouble, trial, and tribulation, you can make it!

There are things you live through while you are in the pit you thought for sure you could never endure. The pit shows you that you are more than you think you are, and you can endure more than you think you can. That betrayal, abandonment, struggle, failed marriage, financial crisis, or bitter disappointment of the pit is bringing you clarity! These struggles are what will show you to you. When you come out of the pit, you will see you in a whole new way.

There are people who will never appreciate your breakthroughs because they have no understanding of your been-throughs! But you do!

> And they took him, and cast him into a pit: and the
> pit was empty, there was no water in it.
> —GENESIS 37:24, KJV

The pit is where Joseph experienced some of the greatest pain of his life. Can you imagine how he must have felt as he sat there languishing helplessly in that pit? Trapped there in the pit, the stinging cruel and hateful reality of his circumstances truly begins to sink in. His whole world comes crashing down on him as he comes to terms with the fact that his brothers had placed him there to die. He was dying because he dared to dream.

The range of emotions that he experienced must have been indescribable to say the least: fear, anger, bitterness, rage, disappointment, disillusionment, and disbelief—all these combined with deep levels of anxiety, abandonment, worry, sadness, and heartbreak. (And this is the short list!) Virtually every negative emotion imaginable lambasted and tormented his mind while he was sitting in that pit.

Joseph was placed in the pit not just to discover his true *self*, but also to discover his true *source*.

The Bible says that the pit was empty and very dry. This tells us Joseph was lonely and thirsty. Certainly he must have been thirsty for water, but let's look a little deeper. His greatest thirst was for companionship in this painful place.

Oftentimes one of the hardest parts of being in the pit is dealing with loneliness. The solitude and sadness of the pit can at times seem overwhelming. Joseph was in great pain, and in that great pain, he had no one. Let's face it; all of us have spent time in the pit, and it goes without saying, the lonely pit is a painful place!

It is easy to question and wonder why God will often allow you to face the pit all by yourself. To be in such a painful place in life can be so difficult, but then to compound the issue, you are alone. In times like this the old saying rings true, "Misery loves company!"

It's somehow easier to endure the pit when you have company. When you have partners in pain and brothers in brokenness, it all seems a little more bearable. But what happens when you are alone? *That's when you must realize that you are not alone.*

Even though Joseph was in the pit, he was not alone. Yes, he was in that pit with none of his usual earthly sources and earthy companions, but he was not alone. God was with him all the time.

There are many reasons to praise God, but anyone who has been in the pit can praise Him because He never leaves you alone in the pit. In your pit places, the only reason you don't lose your mind, throw in the towel, or give up is because, even when you don't realize it, God is with you in the pit. This brings us to the second reason why you cannot bypass the pit.

2. The Lord wants to reveal Himself to you in new ways.

The Lord allowed and even orchestrated Joseph's time in the pit because He wanted to be known in a different way by Joseph.

Remember, the pit was not a place of death but discovery. God wants to be revealed in the pit!

Joseph was placed in the pit not just to discover his true *self* but also to discover his true *source*. In the pit is where God often reveals Himself. One of the names of God in the Old Testament is *Jehovah*. A simple definition of the name Jehovah is "the God who exists," or "the God who is there." So when you call him *Jehovah Jireh*, you are declaring He is "the God who is there to provide."

When you call him *Jehovah Rapha*, you are declaring He is "the God who is there to heal," and *Jehovah Shalom* tells you He is "the God who exists to bring us peace." The point is that the pit does not stop Jehovah from being who He is. On the contrary, the pit is what *allows* Him to be who He is.

You see, He is Jehovah, He is real, He exists, and He is there even though you may be in the pit. The pit doesn't hide Him; the pit actually reveals Him!

There are things that God wants to reveal to you about Himself that can only be revealed in the pit. He created you for friendship and fellowship. He created you because His desire is for you to know Him. And there are certain dimensions of God's personality that can never be discovered without time in the pit.

> The pit does not stop Jehovah from being who He is. On the contrary, the pit is what *allows* Him to be who He is.

God not only showed Joseph to Joseph in the pit, but God also showed parts of Himself to Joseph that only the pit could uncover. And the same is true today. God will allow you to spend time in the pit because He wants you to know Him, not just in the good times but in the bad as well.

I believe that as Joseph sat there in that hot, dry, lonely pit, he probably had time to do some soul searching. He could have asked himself some of the same intense and thought-provoking questions you ask yourself when you find yourself in the pits of life.

Joseph was in a pit, but his destination was the palace. Don't get comfortable in the pit, because you aren't staying there—you're going to the palace. Don't decorate the walls with pictures, carpet the floor with shag, put in a big-screen television, or move in the living room furniture. The pit is temporary, not a permanent location.

Instead you need to anticipate the process and pack your bags, because you're moving out of your pit. But you're coming out of the pit better than you were when you got in it! You're coming out with a greater understanding of who you are as a person and all that God has put in you! And not only that, but you're also coming out of that pit with a knowledge and revelation of God that only the pit could show you. The enemy does not want you to know it, but there is power in the pit!

Praise Your Way Out

> And they sat down to eat a meal. Then they lifted their eyes and looked, and there was a company of Ishmaelites, coming from Gilead with their camels, bearing spices, balm, and myrrh, on their way to carry them down to Egypt. So Judah said to his brothers, "What profit is there if we kill our brother and conceal his blood?"
> —GENESIS 37:25–26

Judah knew his brothers wanted Joseph dead, but he had second thoughts. When he saw the caravan coming with their "Cadillac camels" and "Mercedes mules," bearing their riches, he saw an opportunity to convince his brothers of a different plan. Judah appealed to the greedy side of his brothers and convinced them that selling Joseph was better than killing him. His quick thinking spared Joseph from dying in the pit.

God's destination for Joseph was the palace, not the pit. God had a plan, and He sent this wealthy group of pilgrims to motivate and activate His plan. Judah saw them and decided to act upon this moment to get his younger brother out of the pit.

Judah means "praise." And isn't it awesome that it was Judah who got him out of his pit? Nothing will get you out of your pit the way that praise will. Praise will help you take advantage of a moment when something is passing you by. Joseph could not see the rich caravan from the pit, but Judah (praise) could. You can't see your way out of the pit without praise.

> Don't get comfortable in the pit, because you aren't staying there—you're going to the palace.

There is something indescribably powerful about praise, especially pit praise. To praise in the pit is to declare in the face of pressure and adversity, "My God is worthy no matter what I'm facing right now!"

When Judah spoke up, Joseph didn't know it, but he was about to discover his destiny! His destiny was not to stay where he was, limited by the ridicule and antagonism of his brothers. His destiny was far greater than that, but it took Judah to discover it.

Your destiny is linked to praise.

There have been many times when praise has been the key for my wife and me. It was Judah—praise—that got us out of our pit places. When we were very young in ministry, we went through one of the most painful and dry seasons of our lives. My father, who was our senior pastor at the time and whom we worked for, had a devastating issue with his eyes. We had just come through cancer with him, which he had survived, but this issue took his eyesight. Now a man who had known freedom and independence had to rely on others for virtually everything.

Dad was such a loving and sweet guy. He was a precious granddaddy to our children. He lost his sight over several days. I remember when I went into his office during this process and he was sitting with the lights off, weeping. I asked him what was wrong, and he replied, "I can't see the grandbabies' faces today."

My heart just broke.

I had to take over most of his responsibility in the ministry, and I tried very hard to do my best. Our church began to grow, but there were challenges, especially financially, in this small ministry. During this time one of the main leaders of our church came against my wife and me in a very intense way. The attack we were under seemed relentless. This leader wounded us so deeply we considered leaving the ministry. But we could not leave my dad in this condition.

We were wounded, struggling and trapped in one of the greatest pits of our lives. One Saturday in particular this leader attacked us before other leaders so greatly that we hit the breaking point. That was it. We were shocked, hurt, and paralyzed in the deepest pit of our young ministry.

We came to church the next day, and I not only preached but also led the worship and the choir as well. My wife, Dawn, was on the front row, and this leader was in the choir right in the center of the stage. This person seemed to have so much power, and we felt defeated by intimidation.

Dawn was on the front row, standing during worship. Later she described how she felt, saying, "I was frozen in the pain and the problems." She, right along with me, was trapped in the pit. I was leading worship FROM THE PIT. I was praising from the pit. I was even preaching from the pit!

You haven't really experienced the power of praise until you praise God in the pit.

As my wife had said, she was frozen and felt defeated and

intimidated by the attack against us. But as she stood there, the Spirit of the Lord spoke to her to take one step—just step out from her comfort zone and step out in praise. In those days she was very quiet and incredibly shy (not anymore!), but in faith she stepped out. In that moment the power of the Lord came upon her, and she praised the Lord like I had never seen! She described it as a supernatural praise!

The presence of Almighty God was ushered right into that room through her pit praise. Our church experienced an outpouring like we had never seen. Salvation, healing, peace, joy, and miracles began to manifest! All over that building people began to praise God, many from their own personal pit. In a moment we were out of the pit and into God's mighty presence, and in His presence that day we overcame and found victory from our pit. We went from contemplating quitting to declaring, "We are here to stay."

Realize that if you don't praise your way out, you won't get out. Remember, Joseph's other brothers wanted him dead, but Judah (praise) kept him alive! Even if you have to praise in peril, clap in calamity, dance in a dilemma, or shout in shackles, don't lose your praise! There will be times when praise will keep you alive.

As you prepare to read the next chapter about the different coats Joseph wore, remember: don't praise about the pit—praise about the promise. Remember, *the pit ain't it!*

Chapter 6

Lose the Coat

So it came to pass, when Joseph had come to his
brothers, that they stripped Joseph of his tunic, the
tunic of many colors that was on him.
• *Genesis 37:23* •

I N THE BIBLE AN OUTER GARMENT SUCH AS A COAT OR MANTLE
was usually made of wool, goat's hair, cotton, or linen.
Depending upon weather conditions, it could also be used as
a rug or blanket to keep a person warm, and for comfort, as a
pillow.

In Jewish customs it was considered a valuable possession. In
fact, it was the one thing that was forbidden to be confiscated
by a debt collector or a creditor as collateral. (See Exodus 22:26;
Deuteronomy 24:13.) In ancient days people from all nations
were fond of brightly colored and ornamented garments, and
they wore them for weddings and other celebrations. Kings and
men of rank kept a large wardrobe of these garments (2 Kings
10:22), partially for their own use (Prov. 31:21; Luke 15:22) and to
give away as presents (Esther 6:6–11).

The coat symbolized status, and for the owner, the changing

of a garment denoted a level elevation. In this chapter I would like to focus on the change of garments. The phrase "change of garments" (or "change of clothing") is used three times in the Old Testament (Gen. 45:22; Judg. 14:12–13; 2 Kings 5:5).

In the life of Joseph, every time he was about to go to the next level in his destiny, there was a change in garments. And the change of garment actually represented something. But he had to be willing to change—to *lose the coat.*

Change is difficult for many people. They hate, despise, and resist change. Change never comes easy because it means admitting that what they are currently doing, performing, or believing is no longer valid, up to date, or necessary.

Human behavior is based upon a series of patterns, routines, and occurrences that shape our lives, so it is human nature to maintain status quo. A subtle but powerful force, routines maintain stability. Still, no matter how difficult change may be, the sooner you realize its benefits, the better your life will become.

Everything in life changes except God. The Bible says, "I am the Lord, I change not" (Mal. 3:6, kjv). To change means "to transform from one thing to another, a shifting." Change is necessary for transformation. Isn't it amazing how many people want to be *transformed*, but not too many people want to *change*? But the truth is, you cannot have the one without the other. There can be no shift in a person's life without change.

As a Christian there are certain principles I adhere to. When it comes to the Word of God, His presence, and His power, these truths are realities that I refuse to fluctuate on in any way, shape, or form. Jesus said it best: "Heaven and earth will pass away, but My words will by no means pass away" (Luke 21:33). But as a pastor, I refuse to oversee a church that is bound by religion or routine. If I choose to be spiritually dead, dry, comfortable, and predictable, I will fail to reach a lost and dying world.

If you truly understand the totality of your responsibility as a church and as a believer, you know that your job is to win the lost—and you must attempt to do that at any cost necessary, so long as the Word of God is never compromised.

Many churches have prospered with great success, but over the years they have failed to change with their society and can no longer relate to society's needs. Is it possible the very people they are trying to win they no longer can reach because of a refusal to change? When churches refuse to change, they are in danger of becoming irrelevant in this lost and dying world; it is irrational to be irrelevant. And the next step after irrelevancy is extinction.

> Isn't it amazing how many people want to be *transformed*, but not too many people want to *change*? But the truth is, you cannot have the one without the other.

My wife and I approach modern ministry with this philosophy: *be current but not carnal.* We have learned to embrace change that does not compromise our message. Whether as a church or a believer, you and I will always face transition.

Joseph is a perfect example of this principle. He achieved his potential because he was adaptable to change. He thrived no matter his situation. Though his circumstances were less than perfect, somehow Joseph remained adaptable to change, and because he did, he always came out ahead. He faced the challenging elements to his transition and adjusted in the midst of adversity. His ability to make certain adjustments and adapt to the transitions caused him to elevate, move up, and be promoted.

I also find it very interesting that each time Joseph made a transition, he lost a coat. Every time Joseph changed coats, he became a changed man. Each coat represented leaving one thing behind in order to embrace a new thing. Joseph wore four different coats, and we're going to take a closer look at each one.

The Coat of Immaturity

> Then they took Joseph's [distinctive] long garment, killed a young goat, and dipped the garment in the blood; and they sent the garment to their father, saying, We have found this! Examine and decide whether it is your son's tunic or not.
>
> —GENESIS 37:31–32, AMP

Joseph's journey to his promise began in his adolescence—that place between childhood and adulthood. Joseph was a daddy's boy, and his brothers considered him spoiled rotten. He was a gifted young man, highly favored by the Lord, but his favor drove his brothers crazy. Nobody can get on your nerves like a younger brother or sister. (Just ask my sister, Donna!)

Joseph's first coat was a garment of immaturity, and though some of his antics were probably cute at first, there came a point when it just wasn't charming anymore, especially to his brothers. Joseph had the right motive, but he may have just used the wrong method. Joseph's life was like a beautiful photograph that just needed to be developed. Someone who is immature has not fully been developed. Give them time. You might be surprised at how beautiful they turn out!

Immaturity is a state of incompletion. Joseph was at a place in his life where his maturity had not caught up with his ability. But the time had come when God wanted Joseph to change his coat, and the only way He was going to be able to accomplish this transition and get to the next level in his destiny was for God to push him out of his comfort zone.

There will be times in your life when you will go through things in order for the process of maturity to emerge. No one can skip the process; it is part of life. But for some, those who have been destined for greatness, their transition requires a stronger adjustment.

When Joseph lost his coat of many colors, it was a sure sign to his brothers that Daddy was no longer going to be his free ride. Where was his favor now? How important was Joseph without his coat?

This tragic event causes us to sympathize with Joseph. He was forced to undergo rejection, suffering, and loneliness. But God was up to something. He was using this dreadful occasion to force Joseph to trust Him. Joseph was being developed.

When you go through adversity in life and feel like the security and comfort from others whom you have depended upon is no longer there, where do you turn? What do you do when the people you used to count on are nowhere to be found? What do you do when the brook (source of life) dries up as it did for Elijah? (See 1 Kings 17:7.) How do you respond when a close comrade deserts you, like Demas who deserted and abandoned Paul the apostle? (See 2 Timothy 4:10.) Foremost is this: you must maintain your perspective.

Understand, God *took* Joseph's coat of adolescence and immaturity because he didn't need it anymore. If he did, God would never have allowed it to be taken from him. As painful as it seems, God will remove what you don't need in order to take you to the next level. But you cannot get there if you continue to hold on to your immature ways. He will take away your first coat to push you out of infantile behavior and into maturity.

At first it seems like a great loss when God takes away your coat of immaturity. It causes you to wonder how you will make it. When this happens, God is pushing you to the next level. Whatever you were holding on to—that relationship or situation—if God wanted you to have it, you still would.

God wants to bring you to a place of maturity where He can develop you and prepare you—not just to *receive* a blessing but also to *become* a blessing. It's no longer about you, but it's about what God can get to you, through you, and for you so that you will touch others.

When a trial, test, or tribulation comes your way, God is not so much testing you as He is teaching you; what you will learn in the process will cause you to be able to help someone else in his or her time of trouble. Whatever you go through, God will use to help you.

> God wants to bring you to a place of maturity where
> He can develop you and prepare you—not just to
> *receive* a blessing but also to *become* a blessing.

Did you notice I used the Amplified Bible to describe Joseph's coat? Read it again. "Then they took Joseph's [distinctive] long garment..." (Gen. 37:31, AMP). I like the way it is translated here. They took the thing from him that distinguished him—the thing that made him different and set him apart from everyone else. They despised his distinctiveness. They would have left him alone had he been willing to conform and become what they wanted him to be, *just like them.*

How often are we guilty of despising those who are different in the body of Christ? We want other believers to be just like us, to praise, dress, act, and respond just like we do. So often in the church we frown on God-given distinctiveness rather than celebrating it.

Don't allow anyone to ever intimidate you, cause you to change, or convince you that you are abnormal or that it is wrong to be different. Different is good. There is destiny in your distinctiveness. Joseph's brothers thought that when he lost his coat, they could take his self-esteem, his destiny, and his tomorrow.

They thought the coat made him different. The coat didn't make him different; God did!

Joseph's brothers stripped him of his beautiful coat of many colors. This is extremely significant, because the coat was what they perceived to be his identity. When they saw the coat, they saw Daddy's boy. When they saw the coat, they saw their spoiled little brother who thought he was all that. The coat was a reminder of who Joseph was in their eyes. So when they took his coat, they were convinced that they were somehow robbing him of his identity, that he would be nothing without the coat.

They failed to realize, however, that there was a whole lot more to Joseph than just a coat. The coat was only what he had; the coat was not who he was! In the divine dilemma Joseph was in, he was required to lose the coat, because God knew in losing the coat he would find himself. He would find out that his identity was not attached to what he had but to who he was. A big part of finding himself occurred only after he lost the coat.

You are more than the coat you are wearing. It's not about the car you drive, the clothes you wear, your elite circle of friends, or the social status you acquire. It is more than the evaluation in society from people around you who don't understand your distinctiveness anyway; often they will eventually turn on you because you're favored by God.

Maybe you have been mistreated, lost associations, or been falsely accused, and you attribute it to an attack from hell. I cannot guarantee the source of the attack, but I can tell you the purpose of the attack. God will use circumstances that appear as being badly treated and wrongly judged by others to strip away what you no longer need! Do not allow your past to dictate your future. Lose the coat of immaturity; it's holding you back from greatness.

The Coat of Self-Sufficiency

> Then it happened about this time that Joseph went into the house to attend to his duties, and none of the men of the house were indoors. And she caught him by his garment, saying, Lie with me! But he left his garment in her hand and fled and got out [of the house].
> —GENESIS 39:11–12, AMP

Some scholars have suggested that Joseph was approximately seventeen years old when he arrived at Potiphar's house in Egypt, and he did not enter the presence of Pharaoh until he was about thirty. During this time he probably became accustomed to his position, excelled at it, and forgot what brought him there in the first place—God.

When things are going well, how easy it is to forget who brought you there in the first place—God. If the Lord had not been with you through all the turmoil, tests, and trials, where would you be?

The only reason you didn't lose your mind, give up, quit on your marriage, commit suicide, or backslide is because the Lord was with you through it all. Even when you didn't know it, He was there all the time. Through the good and the bad, the only reason why you have any success is because of the goodness of the Lord.

During this time in Joseph's life the Bible says Potiphar's wife grabbed him by the coat. The second she reached for his garment, God knew it was coming and He was ready. The Lord was not caught off guard. In fact, God was going to use it for Joseph's good and His purpose. It was a divine setup! She may have gotten his coat, but God had his heart.

God was prepared to take Joseph to the next level—a place so great that he would have no choice but to acknowledge the goodness of God. Consider where Joseph was: Pharaoh's palace, serving under the highest command for the king's secret service. Potiphar was the chief bodyguard for Pharaoh. The likelihood of a young humble Hebrew slave securing a prestigious and prominent position (second in command) was impossible in the natural.

In these great days I believe God wants to raise up a generation of people to a level that, in and of themselves, is impossible to obtain in their own strength. God wants to promote people to new levels in businesses, government, and relationships that will influence their society, but those promotions will never been achieved without God's divine hand.

> For not from the east nor from the west nor the south
> come promotion and lifting up. But God is the Judge!
> He puts down one and lifts up another.
> —PSALM 75:6–7, AMP

Time had elapsed since Joseph lost his first coat, and I am sure that he had not forgotten where he came from, but in the natural he did not want to lose what he had. He had a good thing going for him. He had an outstanding job in Potiphar's house, and he was not going to do anything to forfeit his position. Things may not have been perfect, but they weren't that bad either.

What if someone asked you, "How did you get that job? How did you get such a nice house, car, or family?" What would your answer be? No matter how good you have it, you did not obtain it in your own strength. Avoid the temptation of getting comfortable. Despite your success and achievements, God has something bigger and better. God isn't through with you! But to make a change, a transition, to go to a new level, you must face the process. You have to lose the coat. You will have to be willing to submit to the process: take off the coat of self-sufficiency and replace it with a *garment of faith*. One main key to the next season is releasing this one. You cannot stay where you are and get to where you're going.

The Bible says, "But without faith it is impossible to please Him [God]" (Heb. 11:6). God wants to bring you to a place where He does the impossible *in* you and *for* you. I hear people say all the time, "Pastor, I can't do it." Good! Because if you could do it, it wouldn't be God. The psalmist declared, "*Unless* the LORD builds the house, they labor in vain who build it" (Ps. 127:1, emphasis added).

Jesus said, "With men it is impossible, but not with God; for with God all things are possible" (Mark 10:27). *Impossible* means "unable to be done, powerless, or weak." The place of impossibility opens the door to miracles. You must never be satisfied with what is good. The enemy of great is good. God wants to take you to a level of greatness—not just a level of good enough, but *more than enough*.

Likewise, when God moved Joseph out of Potiphar's house and into the prison, He was positioning him for something better and greater—more than he could ever dream or imagine. It didn't make any sense to Joseph at the time. By losing his coat, he was headed for jail time.

> God wants to take you to a level of greatness—not just a level of good enough, but *more than enough*.

Have you ever been in a situation where everything shifts for no rhyme or reason, and it seems as if God is permitting you to walk through something that makes no sense whatsoever? It is in these moments that what appears to be disaster may actually be destiny taking you to another place; you just don't know it yet.

Joseph went to prison, and even there he thrived. He had been in charge at Potiphar's, or so he may have thought, but his next place would require him to lose all sufficiency in self. (God has a way of showing you that you are not in charge; *He is*.) But it was just a place of preparation.

When Joseph lost that coat, he lost his ability to depend on self. He may have lost his coat, but he didn't lose his dignity. While chained in a dungeon, he prospered.

God is able to make you thrive where others can't even survive. That is what makes you special. He will never put you through something unless He's already made a way out.

> And Joseph's master took him and put him in the prison, a place where the state prisoners were confined; so he was there in the prison. But the Lord was with Joseph, and showed him mercy and lovingkindness and gave him favor in the sight of the warden of the prison.
> —GENESIS 39:20–21, AMP

Read the first line in verse 21 again: "*But* the Lord was with Joseph…" (emphasis added). The conjunction *but* should not be overlooked. You need to thank God for "butting" into your mess. Where would you be if God had not put a "but" into your situations? Joseph knew it was better to be behind bars with God than in the arms of Potiphar's wife without Him.

It's important to note that while he was in prison, Joseph worked on the dreams of others. The best way to make your dream come true is to work on somebody else's!

I have observed that often when people go through difficult times that cause them great pain, the first thing they do is pull back from people. They just want to be left alone. They soak in their sorrow and self-pity, feeling confused and abandoned.

Joseph did just the opposite. He did not sit and sulk; he didn't become mad and bitter. He found a way to be productive because the dream was still alive inside of him. In spite of the fact that everything went wrong, he still had a dream.

That's what can keep you going too. It may have been years since God gave you a dream, but you must still believe in your dream! God removed Joseph's coat of self-sufficiency because He knew that Joseph would never be able to get where he was headed through the power of self.

It is a great day when God delivers you from yourself, because as long as you operate in the power of self, you are limited. It's only through His power that impossible is released into your world.

The Coat of Bondage

The next garments Joseph had to lay aside were the garments of a prisoner, the garments that represented bondage. Nothing will hold back a person from their God-ordained destiny like bondage. Bondage is a terrible thing, and for Joseph to go to the next place he had to leave the bondage behind.

To be in bondage is to be bound to something or someone. The word *bondage* actually has in its origin the word *boa*, as in a boa constrictor snake. Someone who is in bondage is constricted, bound, and limited. A person can experience bondage myriad of ways. Here are just a few.

Bondage to behaviors

One can be in bondage to behavior patterns that are in opposition to their purpose. This often but not always revolves around addictions and desires that are negative and contrary to consistent positive behavior that brings about positive results.

Bondage to past failures

A person can be in bondage to their past, anchored to and held back by the failures and in discrepancies of yesterday. They are unable to walk in the promise of today because of the regretful mistakes and sins of yesterday.

Bondage to wrong relationships

Perhaps the greatest and most difficult bondage to break, however, is the bondage of wrong relationships—people who bring you down. Wrong relationships will imprison you in wrong seasons. Rather than nurturing your next level, you waste time nurtuing a relationship you should not have in the first place. I've heard it said, "Association breeds assimilation." You must refuse to be bound by wrong relationships.

Bondage to past hurts

Joseph was in bondage because of someone else. He was in bondage not because of his own guilt but because of what happened to him. His perpetrator was free, but he was bound. Isn't that often how it is? People wounded and marred by the actions of others live in bondage to what has happened to them—that abandonment, betrayal, abuse. It seems that the guilty goes on with life unscathed.

It grieves my heart to see so many in the body of Christ in bondage because of what has happened to them at the hands of others. They live their lives dwelling among the tombs of the past, bound by what others have done to them.

If anyone could have lived his life bound by the wounds of the past, it was surely Joseph: betrayed by his own family, falsely accused by Potiphar's wife, and ending up in prison. Even when he helped the king's butler, the butler forgot him and he spent two more years in bondage.

Whatever your past situation, it is dangerous to be in bondage, because bondage is such an effective *dream killer*. You must believe, however, that it is not God's plan for you to dwell in bondage. On the contrary, your destiny is liberty.

Jesus said in John 8:36, "Therefore if the Son makes you free, you shall be free indeed." The word *free* in this scripture is translated from the original Greek word *eleutheros*. It means to be unrestrained; it means total freedom from all bondage!

Dreamers can and should live above all bondage that would hold them from their destiny. It's time to lay aside the garments of bondage and put on a garment of praise, because you're going to the next level!

The Coat of Authority

And Pharaoh said to his servants, Can we find this man's equal, a man in whom is the spirit of God? And Pharaoh said to Joseph, Forasmuch as [your] God has shown you all this, there is nobody as intelligent and discreet and understanding and wise as you are. You shall have charge over my house, and all my people shall be governed according to your word [with reverence, submission, and obedience]. Only in matters of the throne will I be greater than you are.

Then Pharaoh said to Joseph, See, I have set you over all the land of Egypt. And Pharaoh took off his [signet] ring from his hand and put it on Joseph's hand, and arrayed him in [official] vestments of fine linen and put a gold chain about his neck; he made him to ride in the second chariot which he had, and [officials] cried before him, Bow the knee! And he set him over all the land of Egypt.

—GENESIS 41:38–43, AMP

God removed from Joseph the coat of self-sufficiency and brought him to a place where he would know God was the one who had elevated him from the pit to the palace. Even Pharaoh noticed the spirit of God was on him and God was the one who gave him understanding. God is able to bless you in such a way that when your breakthrough comes, even the world has to say, "Look what God did for him (or her)."

Joseph lost his coat of immaturity at age seventeen, and he didn't receive his coat of authority until he was thirty. He was called at age seventeen, but he wasn't promoted until age thirty. That's probably because by the time he was thirty, he could handle it; he was a different man by then. He had lived a few years, and now he was prepared. Just think of it; he saw his brothers bowing down to him when he was seventeen. But at that time he only saw the part where they would acknowledge his greatness and by bowing recognize his authority.

In his dream Joseph saw his brothers bowing to his authority, but he didn't know what he would go through to gain that level of authority. It was the authority that Joseph walked in that would cause them to commit such an act of humility.

The coat of many colors was not a garment of authority. They didn't bow to him in that stage of his journey. It wasn't until after Joseph went through his transitions that he earned the right to wear the coat of authority. His experiences had empowered, propelled, and prepared him for the dream God had given him.

Never lose sight of this inescapable fact; your story gives you validity and authority.

> In his dream Joseph saw his brothers bowing to his authority, but he didn't know what he would go through to gain that level of authority.

Joseph recognized that God had been good to him. The Bible says, "And Joseph called the name of the firstborn Manasseh: For God, said he, hath made me forget all my toil, and all my father's house" (Gen. 41:51, KJV). *Manasseh* means, "The Lord has made me forget."

Joseph was so blessed and God was so good to him that it caused him to leave behind the hatred and ill feelings he could have carried against his brothers and Potiphar's wife. Instead he chose to let the hatred and ill feelings go. What a lesson to learn—just let it go. Only God can help you become a Manasseh and forget about it.

How common it is for people to obtain greatness, wealth, success, and personal prosperity and yet be robbed of joy, contentment, and peace simply because they cannot let the past go. They hold on to the memories, the hurt, and the pain. They talk about what happened to them as if it occurred yesterday. They hold grudges. I have found out the hard way that you don't hold a grudge; a grudge holds you! Let it go and walk in freedom.

When Joseph's brothers stood before him, he didn't have to forgive them—because he already had. Don't think that you cannot forgive someone simply because they have not asked for forgiveness. Forgiveness is an act of the will and is not dependent upon the other person(s). Forgiveness is not for them; it is for you.

Instead of hating them, he felt sorry for his brothers. He was a new man. God can bring you to a place where you are so overcome with the goodness of the Lord that instead of despising those who have hurt you, you actually love and pity them. This is a true sign of maturity. You will never come to the coat of authority until you are able to let the past go.

> And Joseph said to his brothers, Come near to me, I pray you. And they did so. And he said, I am Joseph your brother, whom you sold into Egypt! But now, do not be distressed and disheartened or vexed and angry with yourselves because you sold me here, for God sent me ahead of you to preserve life. For these two years the famine has been in the land, and there are still five years more in which there will be neither plowing nor harvest. God sent me before you to preserve for you a posterity and to continue a remnant on the earth, to save your lives by a great escape and save for you many survivors. So now it was not you who sent me here, but God; and He has made me a

father to Pharaoh and lord of all his house and ruler
over all the land of Egypt.

—Genesis 45:4–8, amp

Joseph told his brothers that God was behind what had happened all along. God was working a plan for good.

In order for Joseph to reach the fulfillment and the purpose of his brothers bowing to him, he had to lose a few coats. Before you move on to the next chapter about character assassination, take a little inventory of your life. When you think your situation is bad because you have lost some things—relationships, titles, or opportunities—just remember that the Lord is removing those things so He can get you ready for something newer, bigger, better, and greater.

Chapter 7

Character Assassination

And they said one to another, Behold, this dreamer cometh.
Come now therefore, and let us slay him, and cast him into
some pit, and we will say, Some evil beast hath devoured
him: and we shall see what will become of his dreams.
• *Genesis 37:19–20, KJV* •

W E ALL HAVE HAD THAT AWKWARD MOMENT WHEN
someone publicly speaks out their opinion of another in
a cruel and harsh manner. Oftentimes others are left speech-
less and caught off guard by a verbal assault intended to destroy
someone's reputation. That is what is called *character assassination*. It may involve rumors, innuendos, double-talk, spinning
information, exaggeration, or manipulation of facts to present an
untrue picture of the targeted person.

When it comes to character assassination, the individuals targeted may suffer rejection by their community, family, or members of their sphere of influence. It damages their reputation
and may last a lifetime. Such acts are difficult to reverse or rec-
tify, and in some cases, they tarnish their name even after death.

Character assassination is not just an attempt to destroy you; it is also an attempt to destroy your dream.

Joseph was guilty of one thing: being a dreamer. His brothers hated him and his words. They envied the fact that their father loved him. How was it Joseph's fault that he was the youngest son? His coat wasn't his idea; it was a gift from his father. If the brothers had issues with anyone, it should have been with their father and not with Joseph.

They despised and detested Joseph's ability to dream. Their jealousy, insecurity, and failure to recognize God's favor caused them to fall into the trap of character assassination. It is one thing to be talked about, hated, and verbally mauled by outsiders, but when it is your own family, it cuts deep.

When Joseph approached his brothers in the fields, they spoke evil of him one to another. I am sure this was not the first time. When Joseph entered Dothan, where his brothers were shepherding their flocks, it presented the opportune time for them to act out what they had been feeling and discussing over months, if not years. Hatred built up over time and accumulated with a spontaneous plan to dispose of him.

Reuben and Judah were leaders among their siblings, but even they developed a malicious attitude toward Joseph. It is amazing what happens when a group speaks negatively. Those who are stronger become weak. Instead of standing up for Joseph in their leadership roles, they completely lost regard for their younger brother.

Over time the brothers trashed Joseph behind his back so much that when he arrived, their bashing and brewing came to a head. For years they had ridiculed, despised, and disliked him. Their thoughts become words of hate and disgust. When you speak repeatedly against someone, your words destroy your conscience. You not only speak against someone, but eventually, if you are not careful, you also discuss what you would do to them if given the right opportunity.

Hateful words cause you to devalue someone. You no longer consider them worthy of normal status. The more you speak evil, the more likely you will become desensitized. The conversation turns from, "That person is an idiot," to "I'll tell you what I'd like to do to them."

Joseph's dream had no significance to his brothers because they had devalued Joseph. How could they appreciate his dream when they didn't even appreciate him? They threw him in the pit to die, but when a band of merchants came by, they saw an opportunity to remove themselves from guilt and pass the buck.

> Then there passed by Midianite merchantmen; and they drew and lifted Joseph up out of the pit, and sold Joseph to the Ishmaelites for twenty pieces of silver: and they brought Joseph into Egypt.
>
> —Genesis 37:28, kjv

Now this amazes me. The Bible says they sold Joseph for twenty pieces of silver. It is commonly thought that in the patriarchal days a piece of silver represented the value of a shekel in Jesus's day. In a 2003 article, a shekel was equivalent to 64 cents.[1] Twenty shekels, valued at 64 cents, equals $12.80.

They placed a $12.80 value on their own brother. That amount was pure poverty even in that day. Their opinion and evaluation of Joseph was less than the cost to feed a common beast for a week. Despite their cruel action, their assessment and appraisal of Joseph did not determine his worth. You can never allow character assassination to determine your value. Never allow anyone in your life to have the power to tell you what you're worth!

Don't Let People Put a Price Tag on Your Purpose

There comes a point in your life when you must refuse to allow the assessment of others to become the assessment of yourself. The word *undervalue*, according to Webster, means "to esteem lightly, to treat as little worth."[2] You will always have to contend with those in life who esteem you lightly, who don't believe in your God-ordained destiny and dream.

The beliefs, words, and actions of others do not have the power to place a price tag on your purpose. If Joseph would have had a $12.80 mentality, he would have never made it to the palace. Joseph stood there in proximity of his brothers as they bargained and bartered his worth. What went through Joseph's mind when the trader said, "I'll give twenty pieces of silver for the boy"? He must have thought, "My sandals are worth three times that price." Even more, when one of his brothers said, "Sold," what raced through his mind? "That's it? You've got to be kidding me!"

They didn't sell Joseph for money. His coat of many colors was probably worth thousands of dollars. When they sold Joseph for such a low price, it had a purpose: humiliation. They were trying to send a message: "This is what we think of you, boy." Humiliation is a ploy of the enemy, and he will use those who are closest to you to succeed in its offense.

How many people have allowed a million-dollar dream to be reduced to $12.80 because of character assassination? Every day thousands if not millions of adults who heard the words "You'll never amount to anything" as a child are paralyzed by their past and unable to succeed today. What about the insensitive classmates, bullies, and uppity acquaintances who tease, torment, and mock others' dreams? What long-lasting effect do these dream killers have? None if you handle it right!

Know When to Say Good-Bye

Don't allow the faces of the past—those who passed you by, who considered you a failure or the least likely to succeed—to remain in your present. Don't get so focused upon what you lost. Anything that is no longer in your life had nothing to add to your life or your destiny when it left.

Whatever you need, you still have. Don't determine your success based upon where you are but where you are going. Just because people don't value your dream, it doesn't alleviate your obligation to dream it and fulfill it. You can't fit a sixteen-by-twenty dream in a five-by-seven mind.

Anything that is no longer in your life had nothing to add to your life or your destiny when it left.

You must realize that those who turned on you or sold you out were hindrances to your dream and destiny. If they left you, you didn't need them anyway. I imagine Joseph never expected his brothers to turn on him. There are people you think will be with you forever. There are relationships you thought you would have forever, but for whatever reason they turned against you or simply moved on, and now they are no longer a part of your life.

This is when you have to exercise the spiritual gift called "Good-bye." It's when others turn on you and you can say, "See ya later." Joseph did not murmur, gripe, and complain about what his brothers did to him. He never mentions it again. Once it happened, he focused upon where he was going and where God wanted him to be.

Instead of fretting or worrying about those who left you for dead, you need to go to Walmart, purchase a thank-you card, insert a Waffle House gift card, and send it to them, thanking them for leaving you because you couldn't get to where God called you to be if you had to drag them to the next level. Instead of focusing on what you lost, focus on what is left.

> But now, thus says the LORD, who created you, O Jacob, and He who formed you, O Israel: "Fear not, for I have redeemed you; I have called you by your name; you are mine. When you pass through the waters, I will be with you; and through the rivers, they shall not overflow you. When you walk through the fire, you shall not be burned, nor shall the flame scorch you. For I am the LORD your God, the Holy One of Israel, your Savior; I gave you Egypt for your ransom, Ethiopia and Seba in your place. Since you were precious in My sight, you have been honored, and I have loved you; therefore I will give men for you, and people for your life."
>
> —ISAIAH 43:1–4

God said you were precious in His sight. To be precious is to be highly valued and one of a kind! You must never allow someone's opinion of you to rob you of your worth or what you can achieve. Sure, Joseph's brothers sold him for $12.80 and Judas sold Jesus for $19.20 (thirty pieces of silver), and who can place a value upon Jesus? So don't freak out when others sell you out for less than what you're worth! You are precious, highly valued, and one of a kind!

Instead of focusing on what you lost, focus on what is left.

There was Joseph, bound and traveling in a caravan for miles to Egypt, most likely the longest trip of his young life. I am sure he had plenty of time to rehearse the events that had gotten him to this place, probably hundreds of times. He repeated the confrontation with his brothers, being cast into the pit, and then sold like a common criminal.

When he was in the pit, he probably thought it couldn't get any shoddier, when all of a sudden things went from bad to worse. But in the midst of his stressful situation God was working things out for his good. When things go wrong and character assassination assaults you, God is working His plan to get you where He wants you.

Strife Will Make You or Break You

Then the Midianites traders passed by; so the brothers pulled Joseph up and lifted him out of the pit.

—GENESIS 37:28

The word *Midianite* is just another word for Ishmaelite. It means "contention or strife."[3] Think of it—this is powerful—*it was strife that helped Joseph out of the pit.* Sometimes you will not get out of the pit until some strife shows up.

Strife means "opposition, agitation, and anger." Strife will have one of two effects on you: it will make you, or it will break you. It is essential that you understand that strife is the very thing that will be the test of your character. The problem with many is they have the tendency to remain in their pit, burdened down by strife, instead of allowing the strife to build character and shut the mouth of the naysayers and character assassins.

Let's say you are driving down the interstate. You are playing some new praise music, and in the midst of your worship you become temporarily distracted, veer to the left, and cut someone off. They beep their horn and you swerve back into your lane. Then they cruise beside you and glare at you. You give them a look that says, "I'm sorry about that," and they shoot you the bird. Do you get caught up in the moment and lose your sense of spirituality and shoot the bird right back?

How about when someone cusses at you in a moment of strife? Do you seize that chance to get your cuss on? After all, they don't know who you are.

I understand that stuff happens in real life. But if you face struggles, strain, and strife properly and correctly, they can become the fuel that presses you to your promise.

- The strife of your childhood can cause you to make sure that things will be different for your children.

- The strife of a failed relationship or marriage can be used as fuel and motivation to do things differently next time around.

- The strife that you were in while working for a difficult boss can cause you to be different when you get your next opportunity or job.

Strife will either make you or break you. Strife will elevate you, or it will devastate you. It's your choice.

You may not be able to control the circumstances in life, but you can do something with the strife that comes with them. At some point you must learn to embrace adversity, because that may well be the thing that gets you out of the pit you're in. Joseph didn't know it at the time, but strife was what helped him move on to his destiny and dream.

In Joseph's mind his brothers sold him out. Actually the Midianites (strife) were his bus ticket to the promise. I am sure he would have preferred to ride first class. I can appreciate this; I've ridden the bus before myself. But sometimes riding the bus makes you appreciate what is to come. At the time you despise it, but later you will praise God for it.

The process is always necessary to obtain the promise. Joseph was in the process, and the Midianites were actually part of his *answer*, not part of his *problem*. There will be times when you will have to face things and go through things, but when it is all said and done, they are simply your transportation to the next level. What looked like a dead end was only a detour to the next level. The victory is not how you got there, but where you end up.

> For I know the thoughts that I think toward you, says the LORD, thoughts of peace and not of evil, to give you a future and a hope.
> —JEREMIAH 29:11

I love this verse, not just because of its encouraging hope for the future, but because God views things differently than we do. Joseph dreamed a dream. He told it to his father and his brothers, but how it would be fulfilled, he had absolutely no idea. When his father asked him to go check on his brothers in the fields in Shechem, they were not there.

There will be times when you will have to go through hard things, but they are simply your transportation to the next level.

When you dream a dream of destiny, you don't always understand how it will come to pass, where to look, or how to find it. In the process God will send you on a journey that seems pointless or insignificant. You will seek after one thing and find something very different.

When Joseph arrived, his brothers were not there. Coincidently God placed a man in his path who knew Joseph's brothers and somehow heard their conversation to know their whereabouts. The man asked him, "What are you seeking?" This is an amazing question: "What are you seeking?" Joseph was simply following his father's order, but his heavenly Father was setting things up for his dream journey.

When you dream, like Joseph, you won't understand the meaning or the timing. This is where "For I know the thoughts that I think toward you..." comes in. Eventually you're going to show up somewhere, looking for something and it will not be there. At that moment you'll be faced with this question" "What are you seeking?" This is the pivotal point in the process.

If that man had not been there, what would have happened? Chances are, Joseph would have returned home and told his father he could not locate them. But God had a plan, one that Joseph had no clue of. This is when you need to trust, "For I know..." Even when you are in seasons you don't understand, seasons when you don't know, you must rest in the words of Jehovah: "For I know." God is not guessing about your future; *He knows!*

How many times have you heard or quoted this verse but never noticed the verse directly before this profound promise?

> For thus says the LORD: After seventy years are completed at Babylon, I will visit you and perform My good word toward you, and cause you to return to this place.
> —JEREMIAH 29:10

Did you know that before God said, "I know the thoughts I have for you...thoughts of peace," God said, "I'm going to send you into captivity for seventy years for the mistakes you've made"? When a "mess" comes into your life, it can be what delivers you into your future.

Daniel was in Babylonian captivity, and he was there because of the mess the children of God had made. He was a prisoner of war and a prophet for God in a foreign land. The Bible says that while Daniel read the writings of Jeremiah, he stumbled across a passage of Scripture that brought him incredible hope for the future.

> In the first year of his reign I, Daniel, understood by the books of the years specified by the word of the LORD through Jeremiah the prophet, that He would accomplish seventy years in the desolations of Jerusalem.
>
> —DANIEL 9:2

It was Jeremiah 29:10 and not Jeremiah 29:11 that spoke to Daniel. He discovered that God had a plan, and that plan was to return the people back to Jerusalem after seventy years. Somehow the promise of a future and a hope was lost in the process, but after Daniel read the prophet Jeremiah, he understood that God was going to turn it around.

When you begin the process, you are confused and lost, and others will ask, "What are you seeking?" At that moment you have no idea what you are seeking. Again, that is when you must trust the words "For I know..."

However, somewhere along the process, you will begin to realize the pit, the rejection, and the character assassination are not the devil but God. There will come a point when the "knowing shifts."

> And we know that all things work together for good to those who love God, to those who are the called according to His purpose.
>
> —ROMANS 8:28

Paul was saying that over time we will no longer say "For I know...," but rather we will say, "And *we* know..." Something hidden is unveiled. At one point only God knew He was in control, but there comes a point when you and I realize it too. That truth gets down inside of you, and when you're hit by something that looks like a character assassination trying to take you out, you will do more than endure it; you will recognize it for what it is: destiny.

In the next chapter you're about to learn that stress can be part of God's strategy, but first remember: you will not grumble, complain, or murmur. Instead you will find peace in the midst of your crisis because now *you* know what God knows. You're going somewhere, and had the attack not come, you would never get where God wants you. The assassins thought evil, but God thought of your good.

Chapter 8

Stress or Strategy

Now Joseph had been taken down to Egypt. And Potiphar, an
officer of Pharaoh, captain of the guard, an Egyptian, bought
him from the Ishmaelites who had taken him down there.

• *Genesis 39:1* •

E VERYONE IS FAMILIAR WITH STRESS. YOU EXPERIENCE IT IN
varying forms and degrees every day. In small doses stress
can actually be beneficial to you. When stress becomes too great,
however, it can affect you physically, mentally, and even spiritually. The Bible illustrates how God can take your *stressful situations* and turn them into *strategic opportunities*.

I want to reveal something very powerful to you: there is a
fine line between stress and strategy. Many times in life you will
find yourself immersed in what you consider to be stressful situations only to realize that what you consider stress, God con-
siders strategy.

The real test, then, is discerning between the two. Discovering
what is stressful in your life and what is strategic for your life is
absolutely essential. Being armed with the power of this revelation places you on the path to certain victory.

In order to be able to understand the difference between stress and strategy, you must first and foremost comprehend the source of the two. Stress is demonic and strategy is divine. God has divine strategy in place for your success, while Satan fuses your life with demonic stress, attempting to orchestrate your demise.

> There is a fine line between stress and strategy.

In order to gain a greater understanding of the differences, consider the meanings of both words. *Stress* is defined as "force, urgency, pressure, tension, and strain." Stress is that place of stagnation, a place where you are in a quandary of tension and frustration. It's a place of exhaustion but no rest, hunger for resolve but no way in sight to be satisfied.

It is a terrible thing to be under the strain of stress. Stress will rob you of your creativity and burden you down with worry and anxiety. Stress will steal your peace of mind, pollute your purpose, and suck the joy right out of your life. Stress will kill your vision, and if you don't deal with it, stress will kill you!

Strategy, on the other hand is something altogether different. *Strategy* is defined as "a long-term plan of action designed to achieve a certain goal." Stress is designed to kill you; strategy is taking you somewhere. The real way to comprehend the subtle differences between stress and strategy is to ascertain where the experience you're in is taking you.

Stress devastates; strategy motivates. Motivation is a powerful thing, because the word *motivation* is akin to the word *motion*, which speaks of movement. Someone who is motivated is someone who is on the move! Strategy will require motivation, and motivation brings about movement. Someone who is strategically motivated will be someone in motion.

But motivation has its root in the word *motive*. What is

motive? Motive is why you do what you do, and motive puts you in motion! Motivation is the motive for your motion! Strategy will help put you in motion with a motive!

Is the pressure you're under right now ushering you toward your goal or simply destroying your destiny? Are you emotionally frustrated and unfulfilled? Are you perplexed and aggravated about where you are in life, yet you have no plan to move beyond this place? If you answered yes to some or all of these questions, there's a good chance you're stressed out!

Joseph was a man who knew what it was to live with extreme pressure. He had to contend with the ongoing and ever-increasing malicious hatred of his brothers. He had to deal with the stress of being hated so much that his tormentors placed him in a pit to die. Then he was taken on a horrific journey into Egypt in shackles. Then he was sold into slavery and wound up in prison. Can you imagine? And that was just the tip of the iceberg!

What cannot be ignored, however, is the fact that the pressure he was under is what propelled him toward his ultimate goal in life. The stressing brought the blessing. God used his strain for his gain!

Joseph was placed in the pit, and in the minds of his brothers he was placed there to die. In his mind it was surely the pit of peril. But it pays to look deeper into what's going on here...God had him strategically placed there. This was not a pit of peril; this was a pit of positioning. He would have never been in position for the next place in his life had he not been placed in the pit.

Some of you are reading this book right now from the pit—the pit of struggle, hurt, anger, disappointment, betrayal, health issues, or family problems! You are under attack, and pressures are bombarding you and troubling your mind. You are just sure you're in a pit of peril. But as a child of God, don't receive that! Declare that this is a pit of positioning! Never forget Joseph was lifted out of that pit and carried to Egypt because he was in position. What seemed like stress was most certainly strategy. This is an ongoing theme in the life of Joseph. God would change the place of peril into a place of positioning.

Recognizing Divine Strategy

Joseph is taken into Egypt, and there he is placed on the auction block in chains. Talk about stress! A man named Potiphar, who was a high-ranking officer in Pharaoh's government, purchases him. As hard as it is to believe, God was in this thing. Divine strategy brought Joseph to the place where he was. As stressful as his situation may have seemed at the time, he was exactly where God intended him to be. This is proof positive that you can be smack-dab in the center of God's will for your life but not like where you are!

The Bible says in Genesis 39:1 that Potiphar was the "captain of the guard." Deeper study reveals the captain of the guard was actually called "the captain of the body guard." Some theologians believe that this man may have been in charge of those kept under guard, enemies of Pharaoh, political prisoners, and all kinds of folks. But as the captain of the body guard, he could have very well had the responsibility of personally guarding and protecting Pharaoh. This man with this level of responsibility would have almost total and unrestricted access to Pharaoh.

Serving in this capacity required him to know Pharaoh better and more intimately than perhaps anyone in the kingdom. And out of all the thousands of places Joseph could have found himself as a slave...*he finds himself in the home of Potiphar, the captain of the body guard.* Is it stress, or is it strategy?

Was it an accident that Joseph wound up in someone's house who totally knew and understood Egyptian culture? Not only that, but he is also in the home of a man of great influence and who has almost limitless access to Pharaoh. Probably few people in the kingdom knew Pharaoh any better than Potiphar. Joseph is in the home of a man who knew every want, dislike, or like of

Pharaoh. Do you think that Potiphar was probably like us, and when he came home, he talked about work? It is very logical to assume that he would speak of Pharaoh: Pharaoh likes this, he doesn't like that. He accepts this kind of person, he rejects that kind of person, this is acceptable behavior, and this is unacceptable behavior.

Joseph is the head servant in this man's house, hearing this conversation about Pharaoh—not aware at the time that there would come a day when he would be called from a prison cell into Pharaoh's presence. It seems very likely to me that in many ways Joseph may have been in the school of Pharaoh while in bondage at Potiphar's house. What seemed like stress was actually strategy!

By the time Joseph stood before Pharaoh, he knew exactly how to behave, exactly how to react and respond. I believe it was largely due in part to where he had been in recent years before he stood before Pharaoh. He had been required to be on that particular journey. Joseph had to go through what he went through so he would know how to behave when he got to the palace. It was divine strategy.

Often in route to your palace destiny God will take you through pit and prison realities. This is divine strategy, however, because when you go through hard times on your journey, these hard times teach you how to act when you arrive at God's desired destination and goal. God strategically places you in situations that require you to grow.

Have you ever known someone who got to a place of blessing and breakthrough too fast? When they arrived at that place of blessing, instead of being filled with gratitude, they were filled with pride.

This is especially true in the life of Joseph. Had he gotten to the palace too fast, he would not have known how to behave. He would have self-destructed. But the journey had humbled him. The man who wound up in the palace was a different man from the one who started out in the pit. What Joseph went through was not so much stress as it was strategy.

In your life God will take you through a strategic process so you will act rightly when you get to the promise! His first priority is to change you. And He must truly change you before He can really bless you.

Joseph's hardest times were used by God to propel him toward his divine destiny.

There is a great scripture in the Word of God that brings this process into perspective. In Romans 8:28 Paul tells the church in Rome these words: "And we know that all things work together for good to those who love God, to those who are the called according to His purpose." The mind-blowing part of this scripture is these four words: *all things work together*. Work together is actually the Greek word *sunergeo*, which means, "made to cooperate." All things are made to cooperate!

A revelation of this scripture can be absolutely life transforming because "all things" means *all things*! It means anything and everything—high times, low times, times of great victory, times of agonizing defeat, times of attack and times of peace, times when you're on top of the world and times when the world is on top of you, times of great faith when you please God and Ishmael times when you fail to trust Him—*all things*.

The Ishmaels of failure became Joseph's transportation to his next dimension. Even your Ishmael is providing transportation to your destiny—*all things*. That failed relationship, that struggle, that failure, that betrayal, that financial crisis, that unmerited onslaught of attack from loved ones—*all things*. God is so big and mighty and all-knowing that He is able to use it *all* as strategy. All of it *has* to cooperate for those who love the Lord and are called for His purpose!

The enemy desires to use everything he can against you. He desires that you will languish helplessly in the failure, friction, and frustration of your past. But not God. The Lord desires for you to get over it and get on with pursuing His destiny for your life. God will make all things strategic for your destiny. All things will work for your good!

Stress will break you *down*; strategy will break you *through*.

Even as you're reading this book, why not stop right now and review the past seasons of your life—the good, the bad, and the ugly. Look at the pit problems and the prison places, see it all and declare by faith, "I will not allow it to be *stress in* my life. On the contrary, it is *strategy for* my life!"

Remember, stress will break you *down*; strategy will break you *through*. Somebody reading this needs to know: you're not headed for a breakdown; you're headed for a breakthrough! The Lord is saying to you today, "I had to take you through it all to change you and get you ready for the promise. It's all working together!"

Now turn the page to the next chapter, and discover what you need to know so that you don't commit "dream suicide."

Chapter 9

Dream Suicide

And it came to pass after these things that his master's
wife cast longing eyes on Joseph, and she said, "Lie with
me." But he refused and said to his master's wife, "...How
then can I do this great wickedness, and sin against
God?" So it was, as she spoke to Joseph day by day, that
he did not heed her, to lie with her or to be with her.
• *Genesis 39:7–10* •

SUICIDE COMES FROM THE LATIN WORDS *SUI*, MEANING "OF
oneself," and *cide*, meaning "death." Combined, the word
suicide means to kill oneself intentionally. What a tragedy. I can
think of few things in the world more devastating and more horrific than the act of suicide. Suicide is so devastating because it
speaks of finality. It's the end in so many ways.

Over many years in ministry one of the hardest things I have
ever done is walk a family through the suicide of a loved one.
Families are distraught and inconsolable. The one who commits
suicide leaves behind him or her a trail of tears.

Suicide cuts so deeply. It carries with it writhing and ringing
pain; it screams final, the end, game over! A precious family is

left to pick up the pieces and try to make sense of it all. The finality of suicide is so intense because when a person commits suicide, not only do they die, but their potential for goodness, victory, happiness, productivity, and breakthrough also die right along with them. Those closest to them know it, and that causes great pain.

One of the most regrettable and greatest pains is the pain of what could have been but never was. More often than not, the person who commits suicide has lost sight of the future and is caught totally in the misery of the moment.

I believe the most crippling aspect of suicide is that after the person who commits suicide dies, the ones who are still living have to contend with pain every day, the heartache of wondering, "What could I have done differently? Could I have made a difference? Why didn't I see this coming?" They face anew the death of the one they loved each morning; the person they loved is gone, while they still live.

In the same way dream suicide is when you kill and destroy your own dreams. You become so locked into and hypnotized by the misery of the moment you lose sight of the promise that dwells in your future. I have seen many, especially in ministry, lose sight of their dreams and in a moment of indiscretion or desperation commit dream suicide. Can you imagine the fallout in their lives? Great ministry, great potential, great influence, great relationships, great opportunities are lost!

Similar to the crippling aftermath of a physical suicide, the pain of dream suicide is that your dream is dead but you are still alive, and every day you have to face the fact that you were the architect of your own demise. You killed your own dream. It's living in the syndrome of what could have been but never was.

What's even worse is to see someone literally living the dream and then commit dream suicide. Now they live in the pain of forfeited potential every day. That's pain, to live on knowing you killed your own dream. And the questions are the same questions that a family of a suicide victim faces. In despair the person who commits dream suicide will ask, "What could I have done differently? How did I let this happen? Why didn't I see this coming?" Dream suicide is devastating, because the dreamer still lives while the dream is dead.

Experiences of life will have their ups and downs. Challenges, difficulties, and hardships will come knocking on each person's door at some point in their journey. How you face them will dictate how others view you. The trials you endure are God's reconstructive surgery and are to make you look better. However, others may see it differently. At times people will think that if you face adversity or obscurity, you are cursed or you will always struggle.

Don't let yourself become like many other people who face hard times and take on a victim mentality—blaming others, becoming resentful, and thinking the world owes them something for the "bad luck" they've experienced. The wounds of life can leave scars that speak loudly of what you have endured. Wounds that represent what you have been through. Wounds that represent what you have survived. Don't despise your wounds.

> Joseph had a slave reality but
> never had a slave mentality.

You must refuse to allow wounds of the past to sabotage the promise of the future. Never commit dream suicide by giving your wounds the power to make you quit. Your wounds should fuel your dreams and the dreams of others. Because despite all you've faced, you're still here, and you're still dreaming.

How easy it is for people in the church to hide their wounds, to prevent others from seeing their mess. If someone is scarred by an accident, a person may try to cover it with makeup. People do the same thing emotionally; they attempt to cover up their wounds, fearful of what others may think of them. Their injuries, scars, and wounds remind them of where they have been and what they have been through in life's journey.

This was the case with Joseph. He had suffered the hatred from his brothers and faced the ditch of despair and the road of rejection. Yet his path to the palace did more than elevate him in social and political status. His promotion was from the Lord, and the benefits of his presence in Pharaoh's house brought the blessings of the Lord.

Joseph did not hold his head down in self-pity. Instead he continued to see himself in the hand of His creator, a promise with a destiny, a boy with a dream. Joseph had a slave reality but never had a slave mentality. He was a dreamer. His mentality raised him above his reality. Nothing will change your reality as will victorious thinking. God's hand rested on his life, and because of that he was elevated.

He found a way to be a blessing in the hardest circumstances. Even if your circumstances are not ideal, God's blessing on you will ooze on others. Oftentimes the truest test of favor is not how much you are blessed but how much you are able to bless others.

> It is important to see what God is doing
> *to* you, but it's even more important to
> see what God is doing *through* you.

The Word of God says that for Joseph's sake, the blessing of the Lord was on *all* that he had in the *house* and in the *field*. What an amazing statement. When God elevated Joseph, Joseph did not let the promotion go to his head. He did not get conceited or become arrogant. Instead this dreamer recognized that wherever God placed him, he was going to do his task as if the

Lord was his employer. Joseph remained humble, and because of that, he remained blessed. Don't become prideful. Becoming prideful is one of the quickest paths to dream suicide.

The Bible says that the blessing was on *all* that he had. Many times it is easy to lose track of where you are and what God is doing. It is important to see what God is doing *to* you, but it's even more important to see what God is doing *through* you. Because of Joseph, Potiphar's house and field were blessed. Don't get angry at God when others around you get the promotion, the raise, the new house, the new car. Don't covet or become envious.

They are blessed because you still realize you are a dreamer. Where you are now is not where you will stay. If you remain faithful, in due season God will elevate you. But in the meantime, recognize that your presence will bring favor. Expect that others, even those who despise you, ridicule you, or even hate you, will benefit from your company. In fact, when others begin to receive undeserved favor, realize you were placed where you are for this reason. Don't despise the season. Hold your head high.

Everyone will face pain—some more than others. Your wounds should not make others look down on you; it should make them recognize the determination and fortitude inside of you that causes you to never quit, never give up, and to move forward. Find purpose. In the middle of your difficulties you need to focus on process and the purpose of the day of trouble. Behind every disaster there is a dreamer bringing hope to others.

Your circumstances do not need to be the commentary on your past and writing for your future. God is able to cause your hardest circumstance to bring elevation rather than devastation. Your wounds, your scars, and your pain will not turn others off; they will cause them to recognize that God has been faithful and that your dilemma of despair has not crushed you but created opportunities for you to become a blessing.

And it came to pass after these things that his master's wife cast longing eyes on Joseph, and she said,
"Lie with me." But he refused and said to his master's
wife, "Look, my master does not know what is with
me in the house, and he has committed all that he
has to my hand. There is no one greater in this house
than I, nor has he kept back anything from me but
you, because you are his wife. How then can I do this
great wickedness, and sin against God?" So it was, as
she spoke to Joseph day by day, that he did not heed
her, to lie with her or to be with her.

—Genesis 39:7–10

Potiphar's wife made a move. She took advantage of Joseph's
position in slavery. She thought his rejection carried loneliness,
pity, and despair. She thought his circumstances caused him
to be a victim, one who was vulnerable. She was sure he would
want to be with her. However, Joseph did not view his condition
as a curse but as a blessing.

> Behind every disaster there is a
> dreamer bringing hope to others.

It was true; Joseph was in a place of bondage and could have
received some kind of distorted comfort from this woman. After
all, he was a slave who was taken from his world. His situation
had robbed him of relationships, security, and freedom. Yet, even
in bondage, this dreamer never forgot who he was.

Isn't it amazing how often people blame their circumstances
for their sin? They say things such as: "God understands and
knows what I'm going through and what I'm facing. God knows
I need to take this journey I'm on. God knows my heart. I've
been through so much, I deserve this."

But the truth is, God knows just how much pressure you can endure. He knows what will break you and what will make you.

Don't Forget Who You Are

In the middle of your test don't forget who you are and whose you are! Joseph could not shake off who he was. A big part of falling into sin and compromise is when you allow your situa tion to blind you to who you are. Joseph did not lose his identity. Just because he was away from his family, his hometown, and his surroundings did not mean he would allow his situation to redefine who he was.

Potiphar's wife had underestimated Joseph. She attempted to take advantage of someone who she thought was swimming in self-pity. But that was not how Joseph perceived his situation. When you allow your surroundings to redefine your character, you will slip into sin. If you forget who you are or forget whom you belong to, you will allow compromise to enter your heart. At that moment you are in the valley of decision.

The moment you forget who you are is the day you will commit dream suicide. Potiphar's wife could not kill the dream inside Joseph. Only Joseph could kill his dream. Her attempt of seduction was a lure of lust, but it was not enough to destroy his dream. Joseph had to act upon it in order for it to devastate his future.

Too many times people allow their problems to reclassify their condition. A husband loses the interest of his wife because the kids demand more of her time, which in turn causes him to reposition his emotions. Then the woman at his place of work, who shows him attention, may cause him to reclassify his vows and commitment to his children. If he does not guard his heart, he will allow his disappointment to turn into disinterest, and then he will believe the girl at work cares more for him than his spouse does.

You and I are no different from this man. I am a man who is faced with temptation. However, I must never forget who I am. If I remember who I am, I will stay on course. If I remember who I am, I will not commit dream suicide. Who am I? I am a husband. I am a dad. I am a pastor. I am somebody's example, and I am a dreamer. As a dreamer, there are certain things I can and must not do. I know I will face temptation, and if I succumb it can derail my dream.

Don't derail your dream! What will prevent you from compromise? What will stop you when you are negotiating with your conscience? How do you walk away from the temptation to cheat on your spouse, lie to gain a promotion, or yield to the enticement of pleasure? You will overcome when you remember who you are! Too often people who dwell in self-pity and sorrow will convince themselves that they are victims of circumstance and allow their flesh to yield to their desires. The man or woman at your job will not cause you to forfeit your dream. You will. He or she is only a pawn in the hand of Satan to lure you away from what God has for you. You cannot allow your temporary discomfort or disappointments to detour you from your dream and your destiny.

The Bible says, "No temptation has overtaken you except such as is common to man; but God is faithful, who will not allow you to be tempted beyond what you are able, but with the temptation will also make the way of escape, that you may be able to bear it" (1 Cor. 10:13). If you yield in the time of temptation, you have to walk away from the door of escape. God will not put you in a situation you cannot handle. Look for the door, because there is always a door. Potiphar's wife had her eyes on the bed; Joseph had his eyes on the door!

> You cannot allow your temporary discomfort
> or disappointments to detour you from
> your dream and your destiny.

Only you can walk into the trap of sin. It is the lust of the flesh, the eyes of the flesh, and the pride of this world that will cause you to commit dream suicide. Joseph refused to compromise when he recognized that to sleep with Potiphar's wife would not only jeopardize his job, cause him to lose favor, or even potentially be killed for such an act. He recognized how it would affect his relationship with his Creator, when he said, "How could I do this great wickedness and sin against God?" He realized that it was his actions and not *her* temptation that would kill his dream.

It is a tragic thing when your own actions cause you to commit dream suicide. Heartbroken, I have watched pastors and husbands, businesspeople, and folks with great destinies kill their own dreams. They forget who they are, and in a time of carelessness and compromise, they murder their own dream.

You must be careful not to become your own dream killer. What really kept Joseph was this: Joseph never wavered in his commitment to God. Even though he didn't want to betray his commitment to Potiphar, his final concern was his own personal walk with God. Joseph's own walk with the Lord was what ultimately preserved his dream at a time of great temptation.

Joseph had the ability to see it for what it was. It was a trap, and it would have derailed his dream. Dream suicide is a dreadful way to die. How tragic to become your own dream killer. But now that you know how to keep your dreams alive, get ready for a setup!

Chapter 10

Ready for a Setup

And they sat down to eat a meal. Then they lifted their
eyes and looked, and there was a company of Ishmaelites,
coming from Gilead with their camels, bearing spices, balm,
and myrrh, on their way to carry them down to Egypt.
• *Genesis 37:25* •

HAVE YOU EVER ATTENDED A SURPRISE BIRTHDAY PARTY
where the individual celebrated is unaware of the plans
or participants partaking in the festivity? The person opens the
door, flips on the light, and the guests jump out and shout, "Surprise!" Those are amazing times.

One thing I have found out is this; life is filled with surprise
seasons. What do you do, and how do you respond, when life
jumps out of nowhere and shouts, "Surprise!"? If it has not happened to you yet, hold on; your day is coming. Life has a funny
way of throwing you a curveball and wrecking your plans. In
these situations most people ask God the same question: "What
is going on, and why is this happening? This is not what I
expected." In fact, the word *surprise* literally means "a sudden
unexpected event."

One of the things I love most about God is that He is never surprised! If He had a birthday (which He doesn't), you could never give Him a surprise party.

He is omniscient. *Omniscient* is one of the words used to describe God, and it simply means all knowing. In fact, the word *omniscient* actually has as its source two English words: *omni* and *science*. *Omni* means all, and *science* is defined as knowledge.

God has all knowledge. That means God already knows what you have been breaking your neck trying to figure out! Nothing ever takes Him by surprise or catches Him off guard. He knows it all, and that's a fact. God is the original know-it-all!

When you fall, fail, struggle, and trip up, God knows it's coming even before it happens. This is part of the mind-boggling truth of the love of God: He continues to love you even though He knows in advance of your sin. That's love.

It is hard to fathom loving someone even when you know they are going to hurt you, betray you, and let you down. It's diametrically opposed to the way that you want to contend with those who hurt you, disappoint you, or let you down. In fact, I'm sure you would rather distance yourself from people who cause you grief or pain. But not God. He loves every one of us beyond our failures.

Watch Out, You're Being Set Up

Throughout the Bible God used people who were far from perfect, and most had some pretty big issues. David had Bathsheba, Moses had an anger problem, Peter was a curser, and Abraham? Well, Abraham had Ishmael.

Why did I mention Ishmael? There was a divine setup that took place in Joseph's life that started long before he was born. It started when Abraham had Ishmael. Let's delve a little deeper into the background of this story.

You've probably heard the story of Abraham many times. In

Genesis 12 you can read that God promised Abraham he would be the father of a great nation. Years went by, and Abraham and Sarah saw nothing happening, so they decided to help God out. That was Abraham's monumental mistake, assuming that God needed any help!

I have found that God doesn't need my help; I need His! You and I get in trouble when we try to force something to happen before its time. You can do what seems to be a right thing at a wrong time and fail. For example, marriage can be a right thing, but when done at a wrong time, it can be disastrous!

> When you walk in obedience to God, His
> promises have no expiration date.

Abraham decided that time was running out on God's promises—in today's terms we might say, "His biological clock was ticking"—and he embarked on what would signify his greatest failure and lack of trust in the Lord.

In all actuality, he lost sight of a very powerful truth that is unchanging and everlasting: when you walk in obedience to God, His promises have no expiration date. Even now, if you're walking in obedience to God and have not seen His promises come into fruition yet, don't give up!

Abraham failed to grasp that God had it all under control; he thought the Lord just couldn't deliver. He took matters into his own hands and had a child with Sarah's handmaiden Hagar, and they named him Ishmael. The problem is, God never told him to do this. Abraham, God's man of faith and power, the father of our faith, had an Ishmael.

But how does this connect to Joseph? As I mentioned in chapter 7, the Midianites, also called *Ishmaelites*, were the vehicle to Joseph's promise. It was the Ishmaelites who carried

Joseph from the pit into Egypt. They were called Ishmaelites because they were descendants of Ishmael, the son of Joseph's great-grandfather Abraham.

Ishmael was perhaps Abraham's only mistake in his faith walk. And yet God used Abraham's blunder to preserve his own lineage generations later. So what you or I might call an Ishmael (a mistaken deed), God calls a motion detector. Had it not been for Ishmael, Joseph would not have been spared. God can take your Ishmael and make a Joseph out of it.

I'm sure you have Ishmaels—mistakes—in your past, and the devil has been trying to use them against you. Leave it to God. He can take the worst blunder of your life and use it to preserve you. There are failures in your life that you thought for sure would equate into your destruction. But when God intervenes, He can turn it around to preserve you somewhere in the future.

Ishmael represented Abraham's greatest failure. He represented a lack of trust and faith in God, because in Abraham's mind God was not moving fast enough in giving him a son, so he took matters into his own hands and lay with his wife's handmaiden Hagar. The fruit of that union was Ishmael. That's why Ishmael symbolizes Abraham's failure.

But the beautiful thing about God is that He used Abraham's Ishmael, his failure, to fulfill the promise to Abraham and preserve his posterity. Without the Ishmaelites, Joseph wouldn't have made it to Egypt, and Abraham's descendants would have perished in famine. God used Abraham's Ishmael to salvage and save his lineage. Even though Ishmael represented failure, God is so big that He used Abraham's failure to bless him and his descendants!

This is powerful because even your failure can be turned around and used by God as strategy for your life to help you arrive at God's promised good. God can cause even your Ishmaels to bless you! The Ishmaelites were Joseph's transportation to his promise. There is destiny in you, and God is on your side; your future is greater than your failure. God will use the setback of your failure in the setup for your victory!

You are reading this book right now, and you're thinking about a time when you made an Ishmael—when you gave into temptation, when you made a wrong decision, when you handled a situation your way instead of His way. You think that it created a setback that is too great for you to ever fulfill God's plan for your life.

> Even your failure can be turned around and
> used by God as strategy for your life to help
> you arrive at God's promised good.

But God wasn't surprised by it. It didn't set Him back one little bit. He knew it would happen, and He knew that what looked like a setback could become a setup for your destiny. He specializes in turning setbacks into setups.

If you keep trying to handle things in your own strength, your own wisdom, and your own limited understanding, you'll keep creating setbacks. But if you turn it over to God, not only will it keep you from creating new setbacks, but also He can take those past setbacks, those past failures, and those tragedies from your past and use them to set up your destiny and fulfill your dreams.

God Is Listening

There's another interesting point I want to show you about Ishmael. It's not an accident that he was given the name Ishmael. In Genesis 16 an angel of the Lord appears to Ishmael's mother, Hagar, and instructed her to name her son Ishmael. The name *Ishmael* means "the Lord hears."[1] Wow! This is such an incredible revelation of the love of God. Why? Because Ishmael represents

Abraham's failure, his lack of trust and disobedience to the plan of God. Nevertheless, even in Abraham's failure, the Lord was still listening!

The Lord hears you even when you fail Him. The Lord doesn't ignore you or become aloof and unapproachable. The Lord still hears! Where would you be if your failures, shortcomings, sin, and compromise caused God to stop listening to your desperate cries for help?

People will tune you out; even your own family will stop listening to you if you transgress enough. But I have good news for you today: even if you have many issues and Ishmaels, even if you have cut and wounded the heart of God, the Lord is listening!

He is listening to the rebellious teen. He is listening to the struggling alcoholic. He is listening to the one caught in sexual snares and traps. God is listening. Even to the one in rebellion, the Lord is listening! When no one else is listening, God is.

Everyone has Ishmaels, but your Ishmaels are never a surprise to God. He knew they were coming even before they were conceived. He's ready to turn those setbacks into setups if you'll let Him.

According to Genesis 16:12 (NAS), an angel declared that Ishmael would be like a wild donkey, fighting and resisting everyone and everything. That's what the Ishmaels of life do: they fight your destiny; they resist and hold you from God's best plan for your life. The enemy is determined that your Ishmaels will hold you from God's divine purpose and plan for your life, but God's great grace is greater than your Ishmaels!

God can see the future. He knows what can destroy your family or you. When He sets you on course to destiny, to fulfill His will and promises, the pathway may seem unpleasant or disagreeable to your flesh (your human nature). However, if you can rest in Him, knowing He is omniscient and in control, your journey can become the roadway to restoration!

As a dreamer you will take unusual paths to your promise,

you will experience what appear to be setbacks, but in the long haul the promise pushes you into prosperity. In the end you will overcome. Like Joseph, when it is over, you will look back and say, "What the enemy meant for evil God meant for good." What the enemy meant as a setback, God used as a setup.

It is an incredible thing to see God use your Ishmaels. I have seen so many people over the years with great Ishmael issues. And I have stood in amazement as God uses these Ishmaels to become a blessing. I've seen God take the Ishmaels of former drug addicts, prostitutes, backsliders, and more and use them as a tool to help others in their journey. Never forget: sometimes what seems like a setback is really a setup!

Next, discover the foundations for finding favor that we can learn from Joseph's life.

Chapter 11

Foundations for
Finding Favor

The LORD was with Joseph and
gave him success in whatever he did.
• *Genesis 39:23, NIV* •

JOSEPH WAS A MAN WHO WITHOUT QUESTION WENT THROUGH
the most impossible of situations. His story includes times
of unparalleled and unprecedented victories, along with heart-
wrenching, hope-devouring seasons of despair. When you evaluate portions of his life, it would seem that he was anything but
favored. But a closer look would reveal a very powerful reality.
Joseph found favor even in the most difficult of times. That is one
of the essential components in the life of this amazing dreamer.
He was able to make the most of even the worst situations. His
tenacity eventually catapulted him into the fruition of his dream.

All you have to do is rehearse his story, and you can find
favor shining through every dark part of it. Think about it; even
though he was hated by his brothers, he was favored by his father.
Though he was sold into bondage, he had favor in the eyes of
Potiphar. Yes, he was thrown into prison unjustly, but even in

prison he had favor. Favor eventually led him to being second in command in all of Egypt, answering only to Pharaoh himself. Make no mistake about it; favor is something that is undeniably powerful.

Sometimes to find favor with those who matter, you will have to sacrifice favor with those who don't.

Understand that Joseph had favor in every situation with those who mattered. I know this next statement may seem intense and hard to fully get your mind around. But listen closely: there are some people in your life you will never experience favor with. No matter how hard you try or what you do, you will never gain their favor or endorsement. So stop trying.

Favor That Matters

Joseph didn't need the favor of his brothers; he needed the favor of his father. He didn't need the favor of the other servants in Potiphar's house; he needed the favor of Potiphar himself. Joseph didn't need the favor of the prisoners in the prison; he needed favor with the man in charge!

There is a very powerful truth that you cannot afford to ignore as you hotly pursue your dream: sometimes to find favor with those who matter, you will have to sacrifice favor with those who don't.

You need to reread that last statement. It is time set yourself free from trying to gain favor from those who are powerless to help you as it relates to your dream and destiny! If Joseph would have sought the favor of his brothers and had been willing to compromise for their favor, he would have never seen his dreams come to pass.

Ask yourself an honest question: "Am I willing to sacrifice the favor of those who don't matter in order to gain the favor of those who do?" If you are, I want you to doing something. Right now stop and pray this powerful destiny-unlocking, dream-fulfilling prayer.

> *Heavenly Father, in Jesus's name don't just give me favor; give me favor with those who matter! Release favor over my life with the people who can make my dreams come true! I receive it in faith. In Jesus's name I pray, amen!*

Let's take a closer look at Joseph's journey and discover more about how and why so much incredible favor rested on Joseph's life.

> Joseph's master took him and put him in prison, the place where the king's prisoners were confined. But while Joseph was there in the prison, the LORD was with him; he showed him kindness and granted him favor in the eyes of the prison warden. So the warden put Joseph in charge of all those held in the prison, and he was made responsible for all that was done there. The warden paid no attention to anything under Joseph's care, because the LORD was with Joseph and gave him success in whatever he did.
> —GENESIS 39:20–23, NIV

Favor is more than skill, it goes way beyond luck, and it's often undeserved and almost always unexpected. The Bible says that the Lord granted Joseph favor. *Favor* is a very powerful word. In the Old Testament the English word *favor* is translated from the Hebrew word *chen*. It means "grace, acceptance, and good will." In all that Joseph faced and went through, it is important to discover the keys that led him to favor in unfavorable circumstances because God can and will provide favor for you no matter how unfavorable your circumstances may be!

The essential thing that led to the favor and success of Joseph is found in Genesis 39:2 (emphasis added):

> The LORD was with Joseph, and he was a *successful* man; and he was in the house of his master the Egyptian.

Now don't miss that important fact. The Lord was with him. If the Lord is with you, you're automatically in a position of favor. Joseph may not have been where he wanted to be in the natural sense; however, since God was with him, he was in a blessed place.

I love the fact that the Bible says he was a successful man. He had less than optimum circumstances, yet he still succeeded. Bear in mind, he had been sold into bondage and was a slave. Everything about his life screamed limitation. He was not free to do as he wanted, to come and go as he wanted, or even to live the true life he must have wanted. But in the house of limitations he was successful.

The key to the next level is *this* level. Succeed where you are.

Successful means that Joseph accomplished his aim and fulfilled his purpose. Even in the hard place, because the Lord was with him, he fulfilled his purpose. Never forget; if God is with you and you are in a hard place, there is always purpose to be found in the hard place. Don't overreact in the hard place; don't quit, give up, or throw in the towel. On the contrary, do what Joseph did in the hard place—find your purpose! God will not allow you to be in the hard place without a purpose.

Succeed Where You Are

Something very important to understand is that you must seek to succeed where you are if you ever hope to get to where you're going. Even if you are not where you want to be, concentrate on succeeding where you are. Success in one place often opens the door of opportunity to the next place.

The key to the next level is *this* level. Succeed where you are.

Joseph was successful where he was. He never lost sight of the sobering reality of this truth: he needed God. He understood that without the Lord he had absolutely no chance of success, or even survival for that matter.

It's the same today. You might think that your dreams hinge on where you are. But this is how you are deceived. God dreams don't manifest by *location* but by *habitation*. When the Lord is with you, favor is with you, and when favor is with you, success is not far behind. There is no way to overstate your need for God.

It is impossible to experience the favor of God without the presence of God. God's presence released favor and blessing over Joseph, and even Potiphar recognized that there was something special about him. The Bible relates the story so incredibly in Genesis 39:3–6.

> And his master saw that the LORD was with him and that the LORD made all he did to prosper in his hand. So Joseph found favor in his sight, and served him. Then he made him overseer of his house, and all that he had he put under his authority. So it was, from the time that he had made him overseer of his house and all that he had, that the LORD blessed the Egyptian's house for Joseph's sake; and the blessing of the LORD was on all that he had in the house and in the field. So he left all that he had in Joseph's hand, and he did not know what he had except for the bread which he ate.

Now let's zero in on some powerful truth concerning favor here in these few short verses.

1. True favor cannot be hidden.

Verse 3 says, "His master saw that the LORD was with him and that the LORD made all he did to prosper." When the favor of the Lord is with you, there is no hiding or denying it.

> God dreams don't manifest by
> *location* but by *habitation*.

Our entire story of ministry has been one of God's favor. Our ministry began over twenty-five years ago in a church that did not have enough of anything. It was in a rough area of town and was relatively unknown. But even in those lean days we were blessed with God's favor. From a small church we launched a ministry that went all over America and throughout the world.

It's been about sixteen years since we became pastors in Ormond Beach, Florida. We started in a broken-down, leaky, mold-infested gym. Several renovations and two church buildings later we are still walking in the favor of the Lord. Our last expansion was a massive undertaking that cost beyond twenty-five million dollars. This was accomplished in the worst economy since the Great Depression.

The month after we broke ground on our new facility, the economy crashed. We saw families in our church who, up to that point, had been extremely blessed and prosperous lose everything almost overnight. Giving was definitely affected. We went from lending institutions standing in line to assist us to virtually no options. Ministers and friends called me from across America and counseled me to pull the plug on our endeavor. But the fact was, I felt that a man didn't tell me to build it, so a man couldn't tell me to stop, and we pressed forward in faith.

God supernaturally provided two gifts in that season totaling approximately nine million dollars. When we needed resources and with nowhere to borrow, God supplied! Favor! Can you imagine, in a time when commercial building had ground to a halt in the state of Florida, on Interstate 95 a twenty-five-million-dollar project is undertaken? This amazing church building began to rise out of the ground in the deadest economy imaginable. It was being accomplished through the *favor* of the Lord.

People from everywhere passed by our church and were shocked to see this kind of expansion taking place in a horrific economy. But God's favor was on this ministry, and true favor cannot be hidden.

This is very important as it relates to your dream. You must believe God for the kind of favor that will cause your dream to come out of hiding. The favor of God was obvious over the life of Joseph, even to an idol worshipper like Potiphar. And in faith I declare that it shall be the same for you! God's favor over your life will be evident so that your dream cannot and will not stay hidden! Even those in darkness will see and know that you walk in the unexplainable favor of the Lord.

2. The favor of God will involve servanthood.

> So Joseph found favor in his sight, and served him.
> Then he made him overseer of his house, and all that
> he had he put under his authority.
> —GENESIS 39:4

Now this is where things intensify. You almost always think that favor is about getting what you want. But there is a whole lot more to God's favor than that. You are blessed when the favor of God rests on you, and that is undeniable. But I want you to read this next statement very purposefully and thoughtfully, because this is important: God's favor does not come to produce what you want but to produce what *He* wants.

The favor of the Lord always has a divine purpose. It thrust Joseph into a great position, and that position was one of a servant. When you seek favor only for yourself, you become shallow, superficial, and self-absorbed. God's favor manifests with opportunity, and that opportunity is to serve. And real favor should manifest a willingness to become a blessing to others.

> **God's favor does not come to produce what you want but to produce what *He* wants.**

I fear for many Christians in the kingdom of God today. It is now popular and in vogue to claim the favor and blessings of the Lord and think there's no expectation from God on our part. Many claim blessings without giving, breakthrough without prayer, presence without praise, access without intimacy, heaven without holiness, and favor without faithfulness.

One quick side note, I am not attaching anything to God's grace to save us. We don't behave a certain way *to get* saved; we behave a certain way because *we are* saved. In transforming our lives though salvation, Jesus transforms our character and our actions.

And it is true concerning the favor of God. God's favor should have an effect on a person. It certainly did on Joseph. In the very same sentence that declared he found favor, the Bible says he served. The word *served* here in Genesis 39 is translated from the Hebrew word *sharath*. It means "to minister to." The favor of the Lord is greatly revealed through ministry. Joseph served and ministered to Potiphar. This is amazing to me, because Joseph ministered to a man who was totally unworthy of him. This man certainly did not deserve the ministry of Joseph, yet he served him anyway.

At some point in your life, when you walk in the favor of God, you will have an opportunity to serve those who are seemingly unworthy. But here is what you must understand: the favor you walk in is undeserved. Favor is something you don't have a right to, and favor is not earned.

Think about it. If you get in a situation where you need help and someone can provide it, you request it of them by asking, "Can you do me a favor?" Through that statement you're admitting that they are not obligated, nor can you require them to do it. It's a favor, something you don't deserve. It's the same way with the Lord: if you deserved favor, it wouldn't be favor!

This is how you serve people who are unworthy of your service—by realizing every drop of the favor that rests on your life is undeserved. When you do, it becomes easier to serve the undeserving.

The favor of God awakened the servant in Joseph, and it was something that marked his entire life. He served Potiphar, the prison warden, the prisoners, Pharaoh, and finally his own family. Joseph served his way into the fulfillment of his dream.

The favor of God and the fulfillment of your dream will require the servant in you to be awakened. You must be willing to minister to messes (those undeserving) in your life to manifest your dream.

3. People will find favor by finding you!

> So it was, from the time that he had made him over-seer of his house and all that he had, that the LORD blessed the Egyptian's house for Joseph's sake; and the blessing of the LORD was on all that he had in the house and in the field.
>
> —GENESIS 39:5

The Lord blessed the house of the Egyptian for Joseph's sake. The very presence of Joseph brought favor on Potiphar in all of his unworthiness! That's the power of the favor of God; those around and connected to you will be blessed because of God's favor on your life. There are people in your life who will elevate because they associate with you. You bring the favor of God wherever you go! Your home, your job, your class, even your car—wherever you are, God's favor stays with you.

One of the greatest examples of favor is revealed through the story of Mary, the mother of Jesus.

> And having come in, the angel said to her, "Rejoice, highly favored one, the Lord is with you; blessed are you among women!" But when she saw him, she was troubled at his saying, and considered what manner of greeting this was. Then the angel said to her, "Do not be afraid, Mary, for you have found favor with God."
> —LUKE 1:28–30

The angel appeared to Mary and called her "highly favored one." He goes on to call her blessed. Now what is amazing is her response. She was troubled and afraid. Isn't that something? She is not being judged by God; she is being favored by God. And she responds in fear. Never allow yourself to fear God's favor!

The real key to God's favor over Mary is this: what was going on inside of her would bless the whole world! Never forget this: favor gets *in* you before it ever gets *on* you! Today the favor of God is in you! Mary's favor was so incredible it blessed untold masses, including you and me! That's the kind of favor that's powerful!

Joseph had favor on him that blessed the whole world! You may be wondering how. Well, think about it. In a time of great famine God supernaturally orchestrated the rise of Joseph to second in command in all of Egypt. God used him to interpret the dream of Pharaoh and to understand that a devastating famine was coming. Because of the favor upon Joseph, Egypt was prepared.

When Joseph's own family was caught in the same famine, it is none other than Joseph who is in charge of distributing the food! Joseph was able to preserve the Jewish race, from whence the Savior of the world, Jesus Christ, was born! Now that's favor! Don't fear the favor, because your favor is going to bless many others!

Here are five powerful faith-feeding, favor-releasing statements I want you to make.

1. Whatever I need to fulfill my God-given dream and destiny, God's favor brings to me in Jesus's name.

2. I will find favor with those who matter and can help me fulfill my dream in Jesus's name.

3. I will not fear the favor of God on my life. I not only accept it, but I also expect it!

4. The favor of God on my life will help me fulfill my dream and will bless those who are connected to me.

5. I will not try to earn God's favor; I will receive it by faith. I know if I have to earn it or I deserve it, then it isn't favor!

You're about to learn about the times of testing in your life. Now move forward in favor and start by *succeeding where you are!*

Chapter 12

"This Is a Test.
This Is Only a Test."

Until the time that his word came to pass,
the word of the LORD tested him.
• *Psalm 105:19* •

ARE YOU OLD ENOUGH TO REMEMBER THIS ANNOUNCE-
ment? "This is a test. For the next sixty seconds this sta-
tion will conduct a test of the Emergency Broadcast System. This
is only a test. The broadcasters of your area in voluntary coop-
eration with the FCC and other authorities have developed this
system to keep you informed in the event of an emergency."

I remember, especially as a child, watching television and
hearing this announcement. This Emergency Broadcast System
was actually established so the president of the United States
could communicate with American citizens in case of emergency. So from 1963 to 1996 *The Flintstones*, *The Brady Bunch*,
Gilligan's Island, or some other "important" show was inter-
rupted periodically to perform this special test.

The broadcaster would always say, "This is only a test." And
you know what? Life is full of testing times. We all have them.

Some tests are easy, and some are hard. Some we fail, some we pass, and many we take over and over again. No one really likes tests, but the fact is, no one escapes testing in this life.

It's important to understand, however, that every test you go through is not necessarily a monumental crisis. It's simply a test. The teacher never panics during a test, because the teacher knows the answers! And when you go through times of testing, God does not panic. He has all the answers to get you through the test, and eventually *you will pass!*

Joseph, in particular, was a man acquainted with the concept of testing. He was tested in intense ways, and he not only passed, but also he passed with flying colors. One of the most incredible scriptures I have ever read in the Bible as it relates to testing is found in Psalm 105. I opened the chapter with it but will repeat it again for you here:

> Until the time that his word came to pass, the word of the LORD tested him.
>
> —PSALM 105:19

This is one of the most profound things I have ever read in the Bible. Pay close attention to what this verse declares. The Bible says the *word of the Lord tested him.* Wow! Not his brothers. Not the pit. Not Potiphar or Potiphar's wife. It wasn't even the prison! What tested Joseph was the word of the Lord.

Joseph was tested by his dream.

His dream came from God, so Joseph's dream was in a real sense God's word over his life. You must come to terms with this fact: your dream will test you. When you get a word from heaven, expect that word to be tested. If it's not tested, there is a good chance it didn't come from God.

The word *test* is a very incredible and amazing word. A simplified working definition of the word *test* is "to prove by examination." The word *test* actually originates from the Latin word *testa*. A testa was an earthen vessel or pot made from ground brick powder and wood ashes. It was used for melting, proving, and refining precious metals, in particular gold. The precious metal was placed in the testa, and the testa proved its purity. The testa also proved that it was ready to be used.

Every one of us will spend time in the testa. When you get a legitimate word from the Lord, you cannot be surprised or overreact to testing. Whether it is a word relating to your healing, destiny, family, ministry, financial breakthrough, or anything else, testing almost always comes.

Don't freak out if you are tested by the dream God gives you.

Joseph's greatest struggles revolved around times of testing. He was tested in the pit and then in bondage. He was tested in prison and when he felt forgotten. Yet somehow through the testing his dream remained intact.

I am sure many times he felt like giving up. In the dryness and betrayal of the pit and in the bondage of Potiphar's house, hopelessness assaulted his mind in the stinging, hateful atmosphere of false accusation. Desperation and loneliness warred against him behind lonely prison bars, spending years feeling forgotten by the very ones he had helped.

The dream tested Joseph. He may have felt forgotten, but the Lord never forgot Joseph. And I have really good news: He hasn't forgotten you either!

In each testing Joseph dealt with, they were tests; they were only tests. Those times of testing were not designed to devastate Joseph but to elevate him.

There's a Purpose Behind Each Test

Whenever God allows testing, there is always a purpose behind it. And that is something you must grasp in your own situation: every test you endure is purposeful. Let me give you some reasons for testing.

1. A test proves that you have learned something.

Whenever you have had to take a test in school, one of the purposes of the test was to prove what you knew. Nothing tells on you like a test!

A test reveals whether or not you know what you say you know. If you learned the material, you passed; if you didn't, you failed. Look at Joseph's process, because the process that God allowed Joseph to go through contained his tests.

If Joseph would have had an unrestricted, unhindered, untested path to the palace, it would not have been good. He would have probably killed his brothers the first time that he saw them! But time and testing had changed Joseph into a man who had perspective and kindness. He forgave his family and blessed them. This act proved he had learned some things during his testing.

I have been in the ministry now for well over twenty-five years. I can honestly say that the testing I have been through has taught me a lot. I know things now that I didn't know in the early days. I have learned not to be so hard on folks and to cheer for everybody connected to the kingdom. I would like to think the years have made me kinder and a little less dogmatic about insignificant things. I've learned that all of us, and I mean all of us, need a whole lot more than just one chance.

But time and testing have been the price exacted for that kind of knowledge. My times of testing have certainly taught me valuable and insightful life lessons. In my toughest times I have discovered what I already knew, but I have been made aware of what I didn't know as well.

The Lord will allow you to be tested to show what you know and also to show what you don't know. I have learned a lot over the years. However, one of the main things I've learned is that I still have a lot to learn!

How about you? Have you learned some valuable lessons

through the hard times you've faced? If you have, then congratulations! If you haven't, get ready to take the test again!

2. *Times of testing reveal how committed you are to your dream.*

Now I have already established through Scripture that the Word of the Lord tested Joseph. The testing proved how desperate he was for his dream to come to pass. In spite of all the testing that he endured, somehow, some way, he never gave up! The intense journey Joseph was on can be described as anything but easy. The psalmist does an astonishing job describing what Joseph went through. Look at the words in the Amplified Bible:

> His feet they hurt with fetters; he was laid in chains
> of iron and his soul entered into that iron.
> —PSALM 105:18

This is so severe and extreme. When they bound Joseph up, they bound more than his hands and feet; they bound his soul. It is a terrible thing to have a bound-up soul.

I want you to understand the implications of having your soul in bondage. A man is made up of three parts: a body, soul, and spirit. Your body is your flesh awareness. It represents your carnal, fleshly desires.

Your body draws you toward the gratification of itself no matter how debase or immoral. The consequences to it are irrelevant; all that matters is the satisfaction of self.

Your spirit is your God consciousness. Your spirit pulls you toward the things of God. It is the part of you that draws you to righteousness and goodness.

Your soul is your mind, your will, and your emotions. It is your eternal living destiny. Your soul is the part of you that will never cease to exist.

When you speak of salvation, the part of you that is saved is your soul. It is your eternal part. Your body and your spirit war for your eternal soul. So when they placed the soul of Joseph in chains, that represented his eternal and living destiny.

It is very important to remember that a real dream killer doesn't just want to bind you physically; a real dream killer desires to bind up your soul. Dream killers do this because they hate and despise your eternal destiny.

When Joseph went into bondage, each time his dream killers saw it as end game finality. But God has a way of working things out! The enemy wanted to use the hard times to destroy Joseph, but God used the hard times to test him. You may be reading this book right now, and you are facing things you never dreamed or imagined you would face. No matter what your issues are, be encouraged. Whether you're facing health problems, financial challenges, career struggles, or anything else, don't lose heart. Be encouraged! This is a test. This is only a test.

No matter what you're going through right now, determine in your heart that you will never lose your soul over it. In these intense times stay committed to your dream. If God has given you this dream, it will come to pass. Don't *give* up; *look* up!

3. A test proves you are ready for the next level.

That's one of the main purposes for testing, isn't it? It proves you are ready for the next level. Sometimes during testing seasons you mistakenly assume that you are losing ground or at least stuck. But the facts are in total opposition to that assumption. During times of testing you are actually preparing to go to the next level!

In each test Joseph endured, the Lord was actually preparing him for promotion. Many people want to graduate prematurely and get turbocharged on to the next level. However, it's very important to realize that you can't graduate until you pass the test. That proves you are next-level material!

In Joseph's story things are going along pretty nicely. He

had been sold into bondage and found favor and purpose in the house of Potiphar. But remember, Joseph's dream and destiny were far greater than being in charge of Potiphar's home. Joseph could not settle in Potiphar's house, because that was not the dream. Hold on for the fullness of your dream! Refuse to allow the ease or success of where you are to hinder you in the pursuit of what you know the Lord has promised.

There were many times Joseph could have derailed his dream. One of the greatest temptations and opportunities came in the form of Potiphar's wife. That temptation was an opportunity for Joseph to satisfy and gratify his own lust and desire. But the Bible says he refused. The word *refuse* in Genesis 39:8 is translated from the Hebrew word *piel*. It means to utterly and completely reject.

Joseph didn't respond to her with a nice little cute no that implied there was a maybe behind it. On the contrary, it was an emphatic and complete no. His dream was too valuable and important to forfeit it over the dream killer of self-gratification.

Joseph didn't flirt with her, lead her on, or give her a single inclination that he would ever be interested in responding to her proposal. He just said NO! One of the essential components to seeing your dream come into fruition is learning how and when to say no. To say yes to the wrong thing can destroy your dream!

I believe there were a few reasons Joseph was able to stay straight and fly right when wrong was in his face.

First, Joseph evaluated his situation. He took a look at the trust Potiphar had placed in him. Evaluate your situation honestly when you are presented with opportunities that oppose your purpose and can potentially destroy your dream.

Second, Joseph considered the consequences. This is so important: before you do something unwise, consider the consequences. Joseph considered the consequences. Behavior, good or bad, comes with consequences. He had to ask himself: "What could happen if I did this?"

When you learn to consider the consequences, you are almost always on your way to doing what is right. Ask yourself when you encounter chances and occasions to do things that are dangerous to your dream: "What are the consequences?" People have made dream-destroying decisions in their lives because they failed to adequately consider the consequences.

Third, Joseph counted the cost. It may have been a real and true temptation for Joseph, but in the end he counted the cost. Think about what it would cost Joseph to have made this compromise. He would have lost the respect of the master who had trusted him. He would have lost his own self-respect for sleeping with another man's wife, but most importantly, he would have sinned against the God he loved and served, and he would have potentially obliterated his dream.

It is very important for those who have great dreams and amazing destinies to learn to count the cost when contemplating compromise. Is it worth it? Is it worth it to transgress or seek quick fixes in life? Is it worth it to allow sin to control you? Is being dishonest with your finances worth it? Is having a sexual liaison in a sinful way worth it? Is it worth it to lose your integrity, purpose, and potential? Be honest and count the cost.

Is it worth it if it cost you your dream? Remember, great dreamer, this is a test; this is only a test. Pass it and get to the next level. Fail it and take it again, or lose your dream all together. It pays to count the cost.

Remember, the word *test* comes from the Latin *testa*. And the word *testa* in Italian means "head." Without a doubt and with certainty, you must use your head if you expect to pass great tests in life. Joseph was successful because in the test he used his *testa*. Joseph used his head.

It is impossible to overemphasize how important it is for dreamers to use their heads. In times of great testing you will fail if you don't use your head.

You're Closer Than You've Ever Been

Joseph may not have known it, but he was getting ready for the next level, and in times of great testing, so are you! Be encouraged; God is on your side, and He is working through this or any test you ever endure. It's important to get ahold of this reality: in times of testing, God is a God of perfect timing.

Joseph was tested until the right time. Your testing season will be over at the right time. The word *time* here is an incredible word. It means appointed time, set time or due season. God had a set time for Joseph to finish his testing and arrive into his promise. He had an appointment with the fulfillment of his dream. As a dreamer and possessor of incredible destiny and purpose from God, you have an appointment with your promise. Maybe you feel disgruntled, frustrated, upset, and disappointed due to the testing you are enduring. But don't give up.

God has made an appointment with your disappointment. It's only a matter of time!

Even in times of intense testing remember something very important: the tests that God gives are all open book! Get out your book, the Bible, and claim every promise of healing, provision, power, and breakthrough!

> Your word is a lamp to my feet and a light to my path.
> —PSALM 119:105

Every answer to every question in every test is contained in God's Word!

Be encouraged in Jesus's name! You must hold on to your dream! It will come to pass. Don't give up prematurely or stop at false finish lines. It's no accident you are reading this book right now. God is reminding you that it's time to reconnect with the dreams He has given you and press forward as never before!

Don't overreact to your dream killers. Your dream killers are often just God's tests in disguise! God uses your dream killers not to kill you but to test you. Look at some of the people and situations that drive you crazy right now and tell yourself something very important: "This is a test; this is only a test!"

Rather than complaining and giving up, start praising God! Your dream killers are getting you ready for your next level. Stop seeing them as just your detractors, and view them as your dream indicators.

> **Your dream is closer to coming to pass than it's ever been before.**

The very fact that you have a dream requires you to be tested. The word of the Lord might be testing you right now, but there's a really good reason. Your dream is closer to coming to pass than it's ever been before.

It's time to learn Joseph's secrets for avoiding the bondage of bitterness. But remember, no matter what your situation looks like or how intense your circumstances may seem, this, my friend, is a test. This is only a test!

Chapter 13

The Bondage of Bitterness

And Joseph said to his brothers, "Please come near to
me." So they came near. Then he said: "I am Joseph your
brother, whom you sold into Egypt. But now, do not therefore
be grieved nor angry with yourselves because you sold
me here; for God sent me before you to preserve life."
• *Genesis 45:4–5* •

One of the greatest tactics hell uses against
people of great potential and promise is to imprison them
in a dungeon of bitterness and unforgiveness. Those who are
dominated and controlled by bitterness never truly achieve their
dreams because they are caught in a nightmare of the past. They
spend their lives trapped in a time warp of yesterday instead of
dismissing the cases against the ones who wronged them and
then moving on.

When you hold on to bitterness, it is very costly. Bitterness is
a brutal taskmaster. It requires you to spend your time, energy,
and mental power maintaining grudges and nursing past wounds
rather than pressing forward into your destiny. Bitterness is the
ultimate dream killer.

When you are dominated and controlled by bitterness, you will blame others for where you are in your lack of productivity and the frustration of your dream. People who harbor unforgiveness are so trapped by their "then" that they are missing out on their "now."

The sad truth is, all the potential for yesterday is gone, and your greatest potential is in your now. Unforgiveness and bitterness rob you of your now.

When you hold grudges, walk in unforgiveness, and hold tightly to bitterness, you are holding on to pain. Your today aches because of what happened to you yesterday. Your today should be vibrant and healthy, but instead it's full of hurts and pains. You are the walking wounded. This is all fueled by bitterness and unforgiveness. This is why you must learn to forgive.

> All the potential for yesterday is gone, and your greatest potential is in your now. Unforgiveness and bitterness rob you of your now.

To hold on to the pain, bitterness, and unforgiveness of yesterday is to sabotage your today. Holding on to an offense stifles your dreams. You cannot produce because there is great barrenness in bitterness. When you don't forgive the people who have wronged you, you actually empower them to hurt you again and afresh. The greatest relief is found in forgiveness.

That's why in order to see the totality of your dream come into fruition it is of utmost importance that you learn to forgive. As you read this book, you may be saying to yourself, "The person who wronged me doesn't deserve forgiveness." That may be true, but just remember, those who deserve forgiveness the least need it the most.

You are never truly able to forgive unless you see bitterness as bondage. Until you see unforgiveness as a prison, you are destined to continue serving time.

When you grant forgiveness to someone, they may not even care. Quite honestly, your forgiveness may not unshackle them; it may not release them or transform their lives. Plainly stated, they may not want it or desire it.

Your forgiveness may not set *them* free, but your forgiveness will set *you* free! Forgiveness will open up a completely new world before you. When you forgive and move on...*you win the fight!* Withhold forgiveness if you want to remain miserable and in bondage. If you truly want to be free, forgive and live!

Forgiveness Made Joseph's Dreams Reality

Forgiveness was a chief character trait of Joseph that brought his dreams into reality. He was a man who knew how to forgive. He refused to empower the pain of yesterday to rob him of the promise and potential of today. He captured and made the most of each moment he lived in. At each stage of his journey he found a way to rise above bitterness and unforgiveness and walk in the full potential of every season in his life. As I've mentioned a few times already in this book, if anyone had the right to hold bitterness and unforgiveness, it would be Joseph. He would have been a *great* guest on *Dr. Phil!*

Somehow, through it all, Joseph never became bitter. Even more than that, instead of becoming bitter, in each instance he became better. Bitterness will rob you of your full potential of improving and becoming better; people who are bitter and unforgiving are stuck. Amazingly, in spite of all he faced, Joseph never got stuck in bitterness.

By the time Joseph stood before Pharaoh, he had been through thirteen years of hell. He was a teenager when his brothers sold him into slavery; now he is a thirty-year-old man. However, he's not a thirty-year-old *bitter* man; he is a thirty-year-old *better* man.

He decided to forget about all his past hurts and pains. Wow! Rather than harbor it in his heart and ruin the season he was in, this dreamer decided to forget the wrongs that had been done to him.

I know you may be thinking, "How in the world can you do that? I could never forget what was done to me." The best way to explain what Joseph did is by tapping into Paul's writings in the New Testament. Paul says in Philippians 3:13, "One thing I do, *forgetting those things which are behind*" (emphasis added). The word in the original Greek text for "forgetting" is a very intense word. It means to lose out of one's mind, but a deeper understanding is this: it means to neglect.[1]

Paul says to neglect those things that are behind—especially the wrongs you have endured. Neglect means to ignore them until their power to hurt you or hold you is broken! When you do that, you're on the way to the next level.

Joseph's actions were not a declaration that he was not hurt by the actions of those who did him wrong. His actions declared, "I am going to forget about it, ignore it, and neglect it. I am going to focus on and fulfill my dreams!"

I heard a story one time about an old saint of God who had been spoken to very rudely in church by some younger ladies. The very next service she was incredibly kind and gracious to these same girls. Someone came up to this dear woman and said, "Don't you remember how badly they spoke to you and mistreated you?"

This precious old lady looked at the person and replied, "Not only do I not remember, but also I distinctly remember forgetting." She understood the power of neglecting past hurts and wrongs.

Bitterness feeds on pain, and bitterness has an insatiable appetite. Fulfilling your dreams will require you to put bitterness and unforgiveness on a hunger strike. Starve your pain to death. Neglect it until its power is broken over your life.

It might be hard to understand how Joseph was able to do that because he was betrayed and wronged at such an incredible level. Insight is given to how he accomplished this when you define the meaning of the names of his sons. I mentioned earlier that his first son was named Manasseh, "God has caused me to forget." Now let's look at the name of his second son, Ephraim, which means "double fruit."

> Fulfilling your dreams will require you to put
> bitterness and unforgiveness on a hunger strike.

Joseph's first son's name means "forget about it," and then he names his second son "double fruit." He explains the name by declaring that the Lord had made him fruitful in the land of his suffering (Gen. 41:52).

Thankfulness Is the Key

One of the keys to Joseph's ability to rise above all the wrong that had been done to him was thankfulness. It was as if he began to do an inventory of his life, and as he did, he surmised that in spite of everything that had been done to him, he had been blessed anyhow!

Think of it; he rose against the odds and overcame when it seemed absolutely impossible. He had been through many hard times, but he had been blessed with "double fruit." He was like Job; he received double for his trouble, and he was thankful! It was as if he was declaring, "After all I have been through, after all the attacks and rough waters, *God blessed me anyhow!*" Thankfulness is an incredible key to forgiveness.

Dreamers who see their dreams manifest into reality learn how to be thankful. As Joseph weighed what he had faced up against what God had brought him through and brought him to, he was thankful! God had blessed him so much that to hold on to bitterness and unforgiveness would be a big waste of time. Joseph was determined to live now—not in the past.

Throughout your life you will go through seasons when you suffer pain, heartache, and betrayal at the hands of dream killers. However, if you are honest and compare your struggles up against the goodness of God, it will be obvious to you that God has blessed you anyway! In spite of the attacks, in spite of the trouble, in spite of the mess, *God has blessed you anyhow!*

Dreamers like Joseph know that walking into the next season of life requires a thankful heart. God is able to give you "double fruit." Instead of dwelling in the past, neglect it, forget about it, and claim double for your trouble!

Joseph never allowed himself to take on the role of a victim. Even in the rough places in life he was productive. It is awesome to me that we don't read of Joseph wasting his time whining, complaining, and blaming. Joseph was someone who learned to replace all that with thankfulness.

If bitterness is the ultimate dream killer, then forgiveness is the ultimate dream savior. Bitterness and unforgiveness have no place in the life of a dreamer who is destined for great things.

In our next chapter you will learn how not to waste your pain. If you have been held captive by unforgiveness, there is no time like the present to come out of that prison. Lewis B. Smedes said, "To forgive is to set a prisoner free and discover the prisoner was you."[2]

Chapter 14

Don't Waste Your Pain

Then Joseph could not restrain himself before all those who stood by him, and he cried out, "Make everyone go out from me!" So no one stood with him while Joseph made himself known to his brothers. And he wept aloud, and the Egyptians and the house of Pharaoh heard it.
• *Genesis 45:1–2* •

THIS STORY IS FILLED WITH THE DEEPEST EMOTIONS IMAGINable. I can almost hear the wails and weeping from Joseph as he presents himself to his brothers. After he explained how God had favored him and the process, he ran to Benjamin, and the two of them embraced. The Bible says they wept on each other's neck.

Joseph was a man who did not take revenge upon his offenders. He was elated to find his family and to know that his father was alive. How delighted he was to discover he had a little brother. When he revealed who he was, he set the tone. He sent out all the guards and dignitaries of Egypt to be alone with his family. It was a moment that he had waited for. Finally the day of restoration had arrived.

The Bible says Joseph could not restrain himself. In other

words, his emotions and feelings were about to burst. The pain he had suffered was for a cause, and it was right before him. He realized at that moment his pain had purpose. His tears were not due to his pain but were shed with deep passion and compassion on his brothers.

My dad used to talk about crying hot, scalding tears. When he said this, he was talking about crying tears that were full of emotion. Tears that represented something you had been through but survived. Tears so intense that they watered the seeds of new beginning. I have been there and done that.

Have you ever cried scalding tears? These are the tears that water the seeds of your new season. These tears shut the door on one season and open the door to another. Don't waste your pain; use it to unlock your new beginning.

Joseph's tears were scalding tears. They declared, "I'm closing the door on what you did to me. I'm closing the door on the pain of the past." These tears represented a funeral and a resurrection—a funeral for the past and a resurrection for a brand-new start.

> Satan desires for your tough seasons to bring
> such pain into your life that you are nothing
> more than a spiritual zombie with no ability
> to help yourself, much less anyone else.

Joseph did not waste his pain, and neither should you. He allowed it to be the catalyst for his praise. Even though he was wounded, he did not allow the process of his pain to cause him to lose his worship. He could see the hand of God on his life, and finally he was ready to experience it.

I can think of very few things sadder than wasted pain. Wasted pain is when you go through the hard times of life and come out of it with nothing to show for it. Satan is a wrangler, entangler, and strangler! He desires for your tough seasons to bring such destruction and pain into your life that when you come through them, you are nothing more than an inept and shattered spiritual zombie with no ability to help yourself, much less anyone else. But not God. He uses everything, especially your pain. All through the Bible we see example after example of pain equating to progress in the lives of God's children.

Paul said it like this in 2 Corinthians 4:17: "For our light affliction…is working for us." Wow! Whatever you face within the plan of God has to work for you. So often pain leads you to promotion.

Just ask Job in the Bible. He went through pain and in the end received double for his trouble. He didn't waste his pain because it was his pain that led to his awareness and understanding for the glory of God. His wife, however, went through the pain of that season that they both faced and became bitter. She wasted her pain.

The Pain of Rejection

Joseph was a man who dealt with pain on so many levels. He faced the pain of rejection. Think of it. He dealt with the pain of being rejected by his own brothers. They hated him and his words. They rejected him and his dreams. They didn't want to hear anything he had to say. It is incredibly painful to be in a place where you are not heard.

His brothers despised him. His enemies did not sell him out; it was his own family. How painful it must have been; he had all those brothers, but he was the reject of the bunch. His journey from Dothan to Egypt took days, if not longer, and I am sure with every step he felt the overwhelming sting of rejection.

Rejection is very painful, but I have learned some powerful lessons about rejection. Sometimes there is direction in rejection. As hard as it is for you to believe, at times you need to be rejected. When you endure rejection in one place, it actually opens up another place. In other words, it's necessary to be rejected in the wrong place so you can be accepted in the right one!

Bearing that in mind will empower you to embrace this liberating truth: the people who rejected you actually did you a favor! Joseph may not have realized it in the moment, but his brothers blessed him when they rejected him. Very often *purpose is discovered through rejection!* Joseph's brothers had no way of knowing that their rejection of him actually opened up his new season!

Rejection creates a feeling of being unwanted, which then reduces self-esteem. The more intimate the relationship in which rejection is experienced, the greater the damage done, and the more challenging it can be to overcome the effects.

No matter who rejects you or how painful it is, their rejection of you in no way means it's over. A great source of comfort is found in the fact that God loves to use rejects! And if you are rejected by everyone else but accepted by Him, then I have a feeling everything is gonna be alright!

Joseph allowed God to work in his heart, which gave him the ability not to allow the long-lasting effects of being rejected to affect him. Dealing with rejection depends upon your ability to interpret the rejection. Very often your response to rejection has great bearing on your future.

When you encounter rejection, the first temptation is to become wound up in a cocoon of offense. But as a dreamer you cannot afford to do this. You must begin to ask yourself the right questions. And one of the main questions you must ask yourself is, "What's next?"

To avoid internalizing your experience of rejection, you must proactively make a choice to detach yourself from the memories of your experience and, instead, attach yourself to the reality of your unknown potential. That's what Joseph did. Notice, the Bible shows that he never mentioned it again, not to himself and not to God.

The Pain of Betrayal

His brothers betrayed Joseph. He was falsely accused for being a dreamer. The Bible tells us that Joseph's ability to dream came from God. So, essentially, his brothers despised God, not just Joseph.

Jesus warned those who were loyal to Him that if they embraced His ministry, they could find themselves having to choose between their family and their faith. As the hostility of living in a fallen world breaks upon us, betrayal will strike very close to the hearts of believers just as it did to the Savior. Don't be surprised if someone in your own family betrays you; one of Jesus's handpicked disciples did the same to Him.

The most common response to betrayal is anger. Nothing hurts quite as much as being lied about. When someone betrays you, you have been emotionally violated. The knife-in-the-back syndrome has destroyed many relationships. The wound sinks deep and can cause a fear of trust.

The betrayal of family members by lying is one of the most devastating things to a relationship that can happen. Lying is the equivalent of making a withdrawal from an emotional bank account. In reality, every lie will always lead to another lie, creating an endless web of deception. Eventually the emotional bank account is bankrupted, with little or no chance of the damage being undone. To betray Joseph, his brothers had to lie to their father. They had to lie about his death, his coat, his disappearance, and their involvement.

There is no denying that their deception was great, but never forget, Joseph's destiny was greater than their deception.

The Pain of Loneliness

Joseph faced the pain of loneliness when he landed in the pit. It was dark and empty. Loneliness is an overwhelming emotion.

The pit experience must have been excruciating. In the pit he was alone and felt unwanted and unimportant.

I wonder if Joseph yelled and screamed from the pit to his brothers, crying for help. Have you ever cried out but felt like no one was listening? In these times make sure you do what David did and even what Jesus did. David cried to the Lord from the cave of Adullam, and Jesus cried to the Father in Gethsemane. Because even when everyone else ignores you, God hears.

Joseph was just a boy, but at his young age he discovered that even in the pit, God had not deserted him. His dream became a nightmare in the pit. But the same God who gave him a dream was the same God who would remain true. Paul wrote:

> Who shall separate us from the love of Christ? Shall tribulation, or distress, or persecution, or famine, or nakedness, or peril, or sword?
> —ROMANS 8:35

The apostle then went on and provided the answer:

> For I am persuaded that neither death nor life, nor angels nor principalities nor powers, nor things present nor things to come, nor height nor depth, nor any other created thing, shall be able to separate us from the love of God which is in Christ Jesus our Lord.
> —ROMANS 8:38–39

Isn't that amazing? Nothing can separate you from the love of God in Christ Jesus! You can be separated from the love of others but *never* from the love of God. Not even the deepest pit can alienate you from His love, because the Bible says *nothing* can separate you.

> Have you ever felt like no one was listening? Even
> when everyone else ignores you, God hears.

Nothing is actually two words: *no thing!* In Romans 8:31 Paul
asks, "What then shall we say to these things?" Send these things
a message in your life: *no thing shall separate me from God's
love!* His presence is your comfort in a time of loneliness, even
in the pit.

The Pain of Dry Seasons

The Bible says that Joseph was placed in the pit, and it was very
dry. Ironically the pit that Joseph found himself in was actually
a cistern that had been dug in the ground. These cisterns were
deep holes hewn into the earth and even into rock. They were
used to collect water. I have been to Israel many times and have
seen firsthand these cisterns, and they are very deep. When it's
the dry season, they are not just dry; they are bone dry. Joseph
was thrown into one of these cisterns, and it was obviously
during the dry season, because the Bible says it was very dry. In
times gone by there was refreshing in this place, but now it's dry.

His brothers tended their flocks in this same region year in
and year out. Who knows, maybe Joseph had been to the same
cistern in times gone by and enjoyed great refreshing. But here
he is in the same place, and it's turned into a dry place. This is
much like the dry places of life. It's confusing when the place
that used to refresh you turns into a dry place. I have seen people
get in a dry place in their marriage, in their careers, and even in
their walk with God. The places where they used to find rest and
refreshing become dry and unfulfilling. Times like these are not
just dry, but they are bone dry. Have you ever been in a bone-
dry season?

It's in these seasons that you are faced with your greatest temptation to quit. I have watched folks quit on their marriage in a dry place, leave a good job in a dry place, and even fall away from God in a dry place. This is so sad because dry places don't stay dry! Just as those cisterns filled up again with water in the rainy season, God sends the rain of His presence to refresh you in your dry seasons.

Joseph surely felt pain in his dry season, but he did not quit, and because he did not quit, God blessed him. He did not hold his head down, quit on life, or go into a depression. He had a dream deep down inside him, a dream from the pit to the palace. He knew he was going somewhere.

You must recognize that in dry seasons God is still up to something. He is watching over you and preparing things for your future. Joseph endured tough times, but his dry seasons were nothing but temporary waiting periods for God to align his destiny. Don't get frustrated when you go through a dry season, because in due time your destiny will be delivered!

The Pain of Being Underestimated

Joseph faced the pain of being underestimated. He had the promise and the potential to be a world-class leader, but instead he became a slave in Egypt. I have already addressed the fact that Joseph was undervalued in chapter 7. But the reason Joseph's brothers undervalued him was because they underestimated him.

There is real pain in being underestimated. It's insulting, degrading, and frustrating. *Underestimate* is a powerful word. It is actually two words placed together—*under* and *estimate*. The word *estimate* is akin to the word *esteem*; when you esteem something, you assign it value.

So underestimating someone is similar to undervaluing a person, but it's more than that. The person who is underestimated not only has his or her present assaulted, but they also have their future assaulted. To be underestimated is to be told you don't measure up now and you never will.

All through the Bible people who were underestimated did mighty things: Pharaoh underestimated Moses, Goliath underestimated David, and Gideon underestimated himself (just to name a few). Time and time again people such as these finished on top. Why? Because God transforms underdogs into overcomers.

When someone underestimates you, they are declaring they don't believe in you. But listen closely: *God believes in you!* God believes in you when no one else does because He knows the great potential that lies within. The reason He knows is because He placed it there.

People who underestimate you don't have the last word; *God does!* But you must exercise your faith and believe about yourself what God believes about you. Joseph somehow rose to the top no matter where he was because in spite of what others thought of him, he refused to underestimate himself!

His brothers sold him out for $12.80. His brothers could have sold him and his coat for a much higher price, but they didn't. The discount price was to send a message to Joseph that he was worth less than a borrowed mule.

People who underestimate you don't have the last word; *God does!*

Even if you've been underestimated, don't allow the pain and the place you are now to dictate where you will end up. Stop right now wherever you are and make this declaration: "My dream is precious, and so am I." Shake off the pain of being underestimated and press toward your promise. Revisit the dream and see yourself in your future *living the dream.*

The Pain of False Accusations

Joseph faced the pain of false accusation when Potiphar's wife lied concerning rape. What a serious accusation. Joseph was in a real dilemma. His accuser was the wife of a prominent person in Pharaoh's palace. No matter what, no one was going to side with Joseph.

One of the most difficult things to deal with in life is how to hold your head up when you know you are innocent. Her accusation had no foundation, no proof, and no witnesses. But that did not matter; he was guilty before proven innocent.

It is painful, stressful, and hateful when you are falsely accused. Some of the greatest pain of false accusation is the loss of relationship. Joseph had done nothing wrong, but nevertheless he suffered the loss of relationship with those around him. Even with the good he had done, there were those in his life who believed the worst about him.

There's a different level of pain when the people who know you, who know your character and your track record, choose to believe the worst about you rather than believing in you. Joseph was a man of character and integrity, but the only one who knew that was God.

When you cannot defend yourself, let God do it. The Bible says, "'Vengeance is mine, I will repay,' says the Lord" (Rom. 12:19). The truth is, if you insist on defending yourself, God will let you. Don't take issues into your own hands; you'll just end up making matters worse.

There will be times when you endure the pain of false accusation. The enemy is very adept at sending deceivers into the lives of people with great destiny. But read this closely: remember who you are, and make a decision to stay the course of your dream. Maintain your integrity, and you will come out victorious in the end! Never quit because of a deceiver. Refuse to allow a deceiver to become a decider as it relates to your destiny!

The Pain of Bondage

The accusation of rape landed Joseph in prison. Once again he was faced with his pain in the process to the palace. His life was filled with emotional roller-coaster rides. The highs and lows of life can cause stress and worry, but Joseph refused to allow his time behind bars to hold his dreams captive.

Even in jail he prospered. God used this time to protect him from sure death from those in Pharaoh's palace who would have taken matters in their own hands. Many times God will hold you captive to protect you. The ride to the top will include a visit at the bottom. Timing is king. God is on the throne, and He isn't nervous.

Don't get discouraged. Doing good landed Joseph in prison. When you are living and doing right, don't fret when it seems you are held captive. Know that God is working behind the scenes and your day of destiny is on the horizon.

The Pain of Being Forgotten

Joseph faced the pain of being forgotten when the butler let him down. After all, he gave him a word of hope and the last words exchanged were, "Don't forget me." But two years went by before the butler remembered Joseph. This was his ticket out of the slammer, or so Joseph thought.

How frustrating it must have been, waiting, counting the days, hoping for his day of release. Have you been there? Have you sowed into others only to have them forget you in your time of need? Joseph battled the disappointment of being let down by someone he was counting on.

There was a great prophet in the Old Testament named Zechariah. He prophesied during a time when the children of Israel were growing weary in rebuilding the temple. It seemed as if their dream of seeing the full reputation of the house of the Lord restored was in jeopardy of not occurring. It was at this critical time that the Lord brought to the forefront a mighty prophet named Zechariah.

Zechariah's name means, "The Lord remembers." It was as if God was letting the people know that no matter who forgets about your dream, even if you yourself forget, *the Lord remembers!* If someone you were counting on has forgotten you, it's not over! Take comfort in these words: the Lord remembers.

I can promise you this: sometime along your journey someone is going to disappoint you. Mark it down. It's not the disappointment you need to deal with, but the hurt and pain of being forgotten. I know this because I have been there. I called on the Lord, asking Him, "God, where are You?" The comforting words reside, "I will never leave you or forsake you, and I remember."

The Pain of Lack of Recognition

Joseph faced the pain of a lack of recognition. His gift afforded the butler his release. Dreamers are gifted, creative, and productive. In order to protect your heart from the pain of no recognition, you must remember who gave you your dream and why you possess it. It's not about you, but it's about others whom you will serve. The real recognition does not belong to us anyway; it belongs to God.

You must walk in humility to preserve your emotions. Do what you do without expectations, without any strings attached, and with no desire to be recognized. Remember the words of our Lord: "Inasmuch as you did it to one of the least of these My brethren, you did it to Me" (Matt. 25:40).

In each situation Joseph somehow didn't waste his pain. I believe Joseph was a worshipper. The Bible says, "And his master saw that the LORD was with him and that the LORD made all he did to prosper in his hand" (Gen. 39:3). But Joseph didn't just have favor in the good times; he had it in the bad times too.

Then Joseph's master took him and put him into the prison, a place where the king's prisoners were confined. And he was there in the prison. But the LORD was with Joseph and showed him mercy, and He gave him favor in the sight of the keeper of the prison. And the keeper of the prison committed to Joseph's hand all the prisoners who were in the prison; whatever they did there, it was his doing. The keeper of the prison did not look into anything that was under Joseph's authority, because the LORD was with him; and whatever he did, the LORD made it prosper.

—GENESIS 39:20–23

Favor comes to those who are in fellowship with God. Favor comes to those who worship even when they are wounded. The Bible says that the Lord inhabits and dwells in praise. (See Psalm 22:3.) Joseph possessed an ability to take his pain and turn it into praise. His praise came when he was in the pit, sold into slavery, lied about, accused of rape, thrown in prison, and forgotten and left to rot.

> A true dreamer is one who can worship when everything goes wrong, even when he or she has done everything right.

I call this wounded worship. Joseph didn't waste his pain. He remained consistent in crisis and chaos. He stayed true to his dream despite the discouragement and despair. He looked up when everything was going down. He turned his pain into praise and his wounds into worship.

A true dreamer is one who can worship when everything goes wrong, even when he or she has done everything right. I believe some of the most precious worship you can offer God is wounded worship. This type of worship declares, "Lord, I'm hurting, and I don't understand this season. I'm a wounded worshipper, but I'll bring you what I have." That is the kind of worship that confuses hell and moves heaven.

The truest test of a worshipper is how you praise in the midst of your pain. Don't waste your pain. Take each situation and begin to praise your way out. Faithful words and songs from the heart will bring forth healing, hope, and happiness. When you know God is still with you, you can overcome every obstacle in your way. He's worthy of your praise regardless of your circumstances.

The Bible says, "Give unto the LORD the glory due His name; worship the LORD in the beauty of holiness" (Ps. 29:2). That means no matter what, God has been good to you, and you ought to get your praise up to that level.

Your praise level will depend upon your vision; what do you see? That's what God asked the prophets Jeremiah (Jer. 1:11) and Ezekiel (Ezek. 37:1–2). You need to see blossoms out of season. You need to see dry bones as a restored people. Compare your situation to your dream. Your dream will keep praise in your mouth when pain tries to crush your heart.

Your vision will determine your outcome. In your pit, see your parade. In your pain, see your potential. In your dry season, see a rain cloud the size of a man's hand. In your rejection, see your acceptance. In your prison, see your palace. In your despair, see the Lord sitting on His throne, high and lifted up.

Begin to declare the goodness of God based upon what He has promised, not what your present circumstances tell you. Don't allow your pain to determine your position. Don't waste your pain; worship the Lord in the midst of your mess, and watch God lift you out in due season!

Chapter 15

My Dream Is
Delivered, but Am I?

*So Joseph made ready his chariot and went up to Goshen
to meet his father Israel; and he presented himself to him,
and fell on his neck and wept on his neck a good while.*
* *Genesis 46:29* *

WHEN YOU SEE ALL THE PIECES COME TOGETHER AND your dream finally manifests into reality, it's an awesome feeling. What a day when the abstract makes contact. Nothing compares to seeing a hope and a dream that you have held onto for years become tangible and touchable in your life. When all the years of transition finally come together to make sense, all the changes and adjustments were just transitions to position. It's an incredible day when a great dream is delivered. And it's at that moment you must ask yourself some honest questions:

- Am I delivered from all unforgiveness, bitterness, and offense? What about the bitterness against the people who so vehemently tried to derail my dream and assassinate my assignment? Do I have the need to succeed just to show those who despised my dream how great I really was all along but they were just too shallow and unspiritual to realize it? Am I looking for the chance to say, "I told you so!"? Or am I thankful?

- Am I so thankful that I have no predisposition whatsoever to boast in my own greatness and in myself? Do I have so little to prove that I can close my mouth and let the dream do the talking? Am I delivered from pride? The pressing question that demands to be answered is this: *My dream is delivered, but am I?*

One of the first things to be delivered from is pride. Pride is dangerous, because pride is to the dreamer what fire is to a dry forest. Just as a fire consumes everything in a forest, so pride consumes everything—the dream *and* the dreamer.

One of the things that marked the life of Joseph was the fact that he never let the manifestation of the dream birth pride in his life. This becomes evident the first time his brothers stood before him in Egypt. He is their own flesh and blood, yet they failed to recognize him.

> **Pride is to the dreamer what fire is to a dry forest.**

Rather than being insulted and offended, he helped them. He had no need to be boastful or anything else. The fact that they were blind to his dream after it had come to pass didn't motivate a prideful or hateful response.

The Bondage of Blindness

Joseph was living his dreams, and those who had tried to kill his dreams did not even realize it. They couldn't see him or the dream. What could have blinded these guys so much that they failed to recognize their very own brother?

1. They were blinded by intimidation.

All Joseph's brothers saw was a great ruler who had all the power and provision. He was a guy who had everything. They were so intimidated by him that they failed to see who he truly was. In fact, it never even entered their minds that this powerful man was actually their own kid brother. If this was Joseph, he had changed so much they didn't know who he was.

This is very significant, because oftentimes, when your dreams become reality, people you have known all your life will treat you differently. They will treat you like a stranger because they feel as if they don't know you anymore. They fail to understand that you are still the same person, just more blessed and fulfilled.

This is why it is necessary never to allow success to change who you are. As best as you can, you must remain recognizable. Never use the fulfillment of your dreams as a way to intimidate those around you. There are those who will be intimidated by the fulfillment of your dreams, and you certainly cannot stop achieving. What you can do, however, is remain true to you; remain genuine and gracious.

I have found the truest test of a man's character is not revealed in how he fails but in how he succeeds. Some folks succeed, and it changes them so much they're not even the same people anymore. In the big picture, it is better to be a kind failure than a hateful success. You need to strive to succeed, but as you go higher, become kinder, more approachable, and filled with greater compassion. Remember this: people who are intimidators eventually wind up alone.

2. *They were blinded by their own need.*

Joseph's brothers saw only in one singular dimension. They saw him as a source to meet their immediate need. They didn't realize that he was so much more than just someone who could give them food. He was family and he loved them. He offered a connection that went beyond only what he could provide in the natural sense.

It is better to be a kind failure than a hateful success.

Who he was to them was vastly more important than what he could give them. Because of who he was to them, he would give them whatever they needed, and what they needed most was relationship, because true blessings flow out of relationships.

Blessings that come from relationships have love as their chief motivation. These blessings are an outflow of relationship and are the best. Relationship offers blessings that money can't buy.

There will be those in your life who fail to recognize you once your dreams are fulfilled because of their need for what your dream has afforded. Like Joseph's brothers they will stop seeing you as family or friend and only see you in the dimension of what you're able to give them.

3. *They were blinded by their shame.*

In Genesis 42:21 they begin to talk about the fact that they were facing hard times because of what they did to Joseph. They are many years removed from what they had done, but their yesterday was haunting their today. The ghosts of the past were blinding them to the promise of their present. They are in the presence of their brother, failing to recognize him because their lives are riddled with so much shame. They carried the guilt of their past into their present season, and because of that they missed the answer that stood right before their eyes.

Very few things blind you like guilt and shame. There will be those who need your help, who need the benefits that your manifested dream can afford them, and they will not be able to recognize you in your season because of the shame of their own. Joseph's brothers' shame became a smoke screen that hindered them from actually recognizing the opportunity to come out of their painful struggle.

As I have analyzed and studied the life of Joseph, it is easy to parallel the life of Joseph with the life of Christ. In fact, as you study Joseph, you'll discover that he is a type of Christ in the Old Testament. A *type* is a figure, shadow, or example. Joseph's life bears a pattern similar to Christ's.

- Both Joseph and Jesus were loved by their fathers (Gen. 37:3; Matt. 3:17).

- Both fled to Egypt (Gen. 37:28; Matt. 2:13–15).

- Both were rejected by their brothers (Gen. 37:4–5; John 7:3–5).

- Both of them were unjustly sold (Gen. 37:28; Matt. 26:15).

- Both were unjustly tried, Joseph with rape and Jesus with blasphemy (Gen. 39:20; Matt. 26:59).

- Egyptians bowed on their knees to Joseph, and the whole world will bow on their knees to Christ (Gen. 41:43; Phil. 2:10).

- Both were later crowned with glory and honor (Gen. 41:39–45; Heb. 2:9).

Bearing that in mind, it's very easy to see how the three issues that blinded Joseph's brothers can also blind you from seeing Christ in His fullness.

The truest test of a man's character is not revealed in how he fails but in how he succeeds.

So often, like the brothers of Joseph, you can be intimidated when you stand before Christ with your needs. So many people see Jesus just as a great King who is uncaring and unapproachable, all-powerful but totally unattached to their situation. They view Jesus as a stranger rather than a friend who will stick closer than a brother.

How often do you walk in less than what Jesus intends for you to walk in because you are intimidated? The Bible says in Matthew 7:7, "Ask, and it will be given to you." How often do you allow the intimidation factor to stop you from asking?

Break Free and See

There are three key steps to breaking free from intimidation and seeing Jesus for who He really is. Let's take a look at them.

1. You must realize that Jesus is not some aloof ruler who is insensitive and unfeeling toward your situation.

On the contrary, the writer of Hebrews declares, "[He is] with by the feeling of our infirmities" (Heb. 4:15, KJV). In other words, Jesus cares. He never reveals Himself as someone who is not touchable or approachable. I love His words in Matthew 11:28: "Come to Me, all you who labor and are heavy laden, and I will give you rest." There's no need to feel intimidated; He invites you to come, with your problems, with your needs, and with all your baggage. He simply says to you, "Come."

2. You must realize that Jesus is more than a provider.

Just as Joseph's brothers saw him in one dimension, so you and I often see Christ in one dimension. If you are not careful, you will view Jesus only as provider. There are those who come into the presence of the Lord based solely on what He can give them while losing sight of who He actually is to them. It is a tragic thing to seek the blessing of the Lord while having no real interest in getting to know the Lord of the blessing. For so many, Jesus is just a sugar daddy, only to be approached when the going gets tough or when times get hard. They come to Jesus only as consumers and miss the essence and opportunity for what Jesus desires most: *relationship.*

The greatest blessings of the Lord flow to you based on relationship. When you understand the power of relationship as it pertains to Jesus, everything changes.

This becomes clear to me when I look into my own world. I am in relationship with my children. They ask things of me that no one else would ask, but they do it because we are in relationship. I do things for them because I love them, not because of a sense of duty or obligation, but simply based on love. If I responded to them based on duty or obligation, then I would fulfill the absolute minimum.

But because of my love for them, because of relationship, because of what they are to me and what they mean to me I go *overboard* in blessing them. It is not because they earned it, not because I owe it, not even because they asked for it. I bless them because I love them. I am so much more to them than just a provider; I am their daddy, and I am in relationship with them.

If you ever grasp the power of relationship as it relates to Jesus, look out. It will make you hungry to pray, hungry to worship, and hungry to spend time with the Lord. The greatest blessings from Jesus flow to you because of relationship. You ask things of Him that can only be asked because of the power of relationship.

> It is a tragic thing to seek the blessing of the Lord while having no real interest in getting to know the Lord of the blessing.

This becomes obvious when you ask things of Christ that you don't deserve, and He gives them to you anyhow. I know in my own life that I walk in a lot of what I call "anyhow blessings"—blessings that I don't deserve but I have them anyhow! Jesus doesn't respond to you based on your worthiness or your rightfulness to the blessing. He responds to you because of your relationship with Him.

Your relationship with Jesus must have its foundation in mutual love, not things. I want you to know and love the Lord in such a way that the blessings become a side benefit and your relationship takes center stage. I pray that your need never blinds you to all Jesus can be to you.

3. You cannot let the shame of your past blind you from seeing Jesus.

Just as Joseph's brothers were blinded by their shame, how often are you blinded by yours? The shame of your past, the shame of your failures, and the shame of your issues can blind you from seeing your answer. So many people are blinded to Jesus because they live in a cloud of guilt that hinders their ability to see Christ. It is a terrible thing to stand before the doorway of new beginnings and find it blocked by blemishes from your past.

To feel shame is natural, but to allow it to separate you from Christ is tragic. To allow shame to separate you from Christ is to assume that you could ever be good enough to approach Jesus.

This type of thinking is flawed because nothing you have ever done can deny you access to Him, and nothing you could ever do can grant it. You come to Jesus based on one premise, and that premise is grace alone. You must shake the shame of your past and boldly come before the Lord, throwing yourself on the unstoppable force of His great grace.

The process of the dream can take years to manifest. It can be a grueling, difficult, and demanding season. It is filled with strife, conflict, character assassination, dream killers, rejection, and sorrow. The pain of the process eases when the purpose of the process unfolds.

You will rejoice when it comes and when the fulfillment arrives. But in the process, don't become bitter. When the dream is delivered, so should you be. Recognize God's favor and forgive during the journey, not when it ends.

Joseph was reunited with his family. He preserved the life of future generations, and today we celebrate the benefits of his dream. Joseph overcame the dream killers in his life, and so can you! Be encouraged, dreamer. Don't give up; *look up!* God's plans for you are wrapped up in your dreams...so get busy!

Dream again, dream big, dream often, dream in color, and dream now!

Chapter 16

The Dreamer's
Survival Guide

"No weapon formed against you shall prosper, and every tongue
which rises against you in judgment you shall condemn.
This is the heritage of the servants of the LORD, and
their righteousness is from Me," says the LORD.
• *Isaiah 54:17* •

THERE IS SOMETHING TO BE SAID FOR SURVIVING. SURVIVORS
make it through what kills others. Survivors live to fight
another day. Survivors keep dreaming even when the odds are
stacked against them. Survivors don't know the meaning of the
word *quit*. Never forget this fact: *you are a survivor.*

Regardless of how you feel or what your condition is, you are
still alive, and you are still here. That makes you a survivor. But
here is something you must know: Satan really does not care if
you survive as long as your dream does not. If you live unfulfilled, unhappy, and dreamless, the enemy is given much joy. But
that is not God's plan, nor is it your purpose. Not only must you
survive, but also your dream has to live right along with you.

In this chapter I want to equip you with the necessary tools you will need to survive the attack of any and all dream killers in your life. This is a literal survival guide empowering you to overcome. If you will put these principles into action, you will see your God-given dreams manifest into reality.

> **Satan really does not care if you survive as long as your dream does not.**

Prepare to discover that God's Word is absolutely true. What was spoken through His prophet Isaiah in the quote at the beginning of this chapter works in your life. Isn't that scripture just awesome? Pay really close attention to what it says: "No weapon formed." In other words, you cannot be surprised when weapons are formed.

As a believer and great dreamer, it is a given that the enemy, Satan, will form weapons against you. It goes with the territory.

Dream killers also form weapons, and that is another foregone conclusion. Where faith kicks in is when you know that the enemies of your dreams can form any and all weapons against you they desire. They can create them and even launch them. But your promise is this: no weapon shall prosper!

That's good news!

One of the most amazing things about Joseph was that he was a survivor. He made it through what would have been certain destruction for most. He had to have had principles that he lived his life by that ensured his existence through the toughest of times.

When you live your life by principles, you are creating the atmosphere for success and victory to manifest. The word *principle* is an amazing word. The Mac dictionary defines principle in a powerful way: "a fundamental truth or proposition that serves as the foundation for a system of belief or behavior or for a chain of reasoning."

Living the principled life means that there are certain beliefs and behaviors that you apply to your everyday life. The principled life is a disciplined life. It's not always the easiest life, but it is the life that will yield the manifestation of your greatest dreams.

For the rest of this chapter I'm going to give you power principles that will help you see your dream become a reality. This is the chapter your dream killer wishes you would not read.

Seven Power Principles

1. Understand the necessity of flexibility.

Sometimes your greatest ability is flexibility. Conversely, one of the most effective dream killers is inflexibility.

In life, and in the pursuit of your dream, you have to be willing to bend. If you are not willing to bend, then go ahead and be prepared, for you will surly break. People who are inflexible often major in the minors and minor in the majors. They get so caught up in the moment or in their own opinions or ideas. Inflexible people lose sight of the bigger picture.

The most inflexible people always kill their own dreams. Now this next statement is something you cannot afford to ignore, because this is a true revelation of the origin of inflexibility: inflexibility has its foundation in *pride*.

I mentioned pride briefly in the last chapter, but let me add here that the Bible says in Proverbs 16:18, "Pride goes before destruction." It is the predecessor of great problems. The most inflexible people are filled with excessive pride. When someone is filled with pride, they see themselves and their opinions as the center of the universe. One of the solutions to some of your most intense problems is learning to be flexible and adaptable.

Being flexible does not mean that you compromise your dream; on the contrary, it means you are doing what it takes to ensure your dream comes into fruition. Imagine where Joseph would have wound up if he would not have learned the art of flexibility. Through each stage of his journey, from the pit to Potiphar's house to prison to the palace, it is obvious that Joseph understood flexibility.

Never undervalue flexibility. Businesses fail, churches close, marriages crumble, and relationships are lost because of the culprit of inflexibility. Don't allow inflexibility to kill your dream.

Flexible people don't break under pressure; they bend. Flexible people bounce back. Flexible people see their dreams come true. Just ask Joseph!

2. Be motivated by faith rather than imprisoned by fear.

Fear is one of the most successful dream killers known to man. When you live your life motivated by fear, you will never see the fulfillment of your big dreams. Without question, a great dream will require you to overcome fear.

There are several characteristics that identify the dreamer who is controlled by fear.

First, fear paralyzes a person in their problem. People who are imprisoned by fear are usually stuck in their situation and unable to move forward. If you allow yourself to be imprisoned by where you are, you will never get to where God has called you to go. Your dream requires motion and movement.

Could you imagine if Joseph would have been dominated and controlled by fear? Obviously he overcame fear, because in each situation he was in, he excelled and pressed as high as he could. He was put in charge of the house of Potiphar, where he started as a slave. When he was put in prison, he wound up running the whole place. Then given the right opportunity, he finds himself second in command in all of Egypt, answering only to Pharaoh himself.

It's important for you to not allow yourself to be paralyzed by fear. Your next level hinges on stepping out in faith, and stepping out requires movement.

- Make the call.

- Start the business.

- Apply for the job.

- Get the degree.

- Start the relationship.

Whatever your dream is, it's time to overcome fear and get moving!

Second, fear will cause you to become comfortable and accepting of the status quo. Fear will cause you to think that you could never achieve or be more, and where you are is just fine. But God doesn't give you dreams that are status quo; you do that just fine all by yourself.

When God gives a dream, there is always something wonderful and unusual attached to it. You serve a boundless, limitless, infinite God. Why would He give you dreams that are just status quo? Living the status quo life says, "Don't rock the boat. Don't make any changes, and don't attempt anything new or different." Who wants to live like that? Not me! But many wind up doing it.

There wasn't one thing about Joseph that was status quo. He was out of the box, a thinker, an organizer, and a risk taker. Big dreamers who achieve big dreams at some point in life have to take big risks.

Being imprisoned by the status quo is an incredible dream killer, and don't you forget it.

The very fact that you're reading this book tells me that you have been called by God to do great things. It tells me that you have big dreams and you are called to live beyond mediocrity. In order to break the status quo off your life and realize your dream, you are going to be required to take initiative right where you are. Don't allow the fear of not doing the right thing cause you to do nothing!

You may be thinking, "What if I fail?" And my answer to that question is to tell you that a big part of prevailing is failing. Don't overreact to failure. You learn to succeed by failing! Your success is often wrapped up in failure.

Don't allow yourself to become comfortable and accepting of the status quo. Your dream invites you to be so much more.

Third, fear causes you to resist change. Change often requires you to step out into the unknown. Change is a reality that everyone must contend with. Great dreamers who do great things have learned to embrace seasons of change.

Joseph was a grade-A, prime-time, real-deal example of someone who made the most of change. It is obvious that most of the changes he went through he didn't like. Who likes living in an atmosphere of stress and hate? Who likes being thrown into a pit? Who likes being sold into slavery? Who enjoys prison? Can you say nobody? Nobody normal at least!

Joseph found success, and his dreams came true because he learned not to fear change but to embrace it. Fear of change will kill your dreams.

Big dreams require big change. You can fret over change, you can fear change, and you can even fight change. But one thing you cannot do—you cannot stop change.

Decide right now to refuse to be imprisoned by fear. Paul wrote a letter to his young son in the faith. In this letter he reminded Timothy of a very important fact.

> For God has not given us a spirit of fear, but of power and of love and of a sound mind.
>
> —2 TIMOTHY 1:7

Realize that God never gave you fear. God gives FAITH! Fear has a source, and faith has a source. Fear comes from the enemy; faith comes from God.

> God has dealt to each one a measure of faith.
> —ROMANS 12:3

I love the word *measure* from the Greek text of the original language of the New Testament. The word for "measure" is the Greek word *metron*. It means the required measure, what is due and the perfect portion! God has given you all the faith you need to fulfill your dream.

There are times when it seems very intense and that your dream will never come true, times when you wonder if you have enough faith. Let me put your mind at ease. You do. But read this very closely: you have all you need, and you will need all you have!

There will be times when you have to access all the faith you have inside you to move forward into God's great dream for your life. But it's there; you just need to use it! Be motivated by faith rather than imprisoned by fear.

You kill the dream killer of fear when you operate in faith!

3. Get over what's over.

I know I talk about getting past the past in this book. But I just want to remind you, get over what's over.

Part of your breakthrough is learning how to *get* through.

You must never allow the past to become shackles that hold you from your future. It really pays to move on. This is a lesson that I am learning in life. Let whatever is over be over. It is freeing. Let it be over for others, and let it be over for yourself.

Understand that, when you live in the bitterness of then, you miss the blessing of now and forfeit the breakthrough of what's next. Part of your breakthrough is learning how to *get* through.

- Get through with the hurt.

- Get through with beating yourself up for your failures.

- Get through with looking back!

- Get through with regret.

The greatest revenge you can exact on regret is to move forward and fulfill your dream! Let all the people you have imprisoned in the cage of your mind go free. When you set them free, it will set you free!

Joseph had to get over what was over to move forward, and because he did, his dreams came true. Get over what's over; your dream is intact, and the best is yet to come!

4. Turn your obstacles into opportunities.

This is so important! One of the greatest keys to surviving the obstacles that rise up and try to kill your dreams is to view them differently. Begin to see obstacles as opportunities. When you do this, you are on the path to success.

There will always be obstacles to contend with as you pursue your God-given dreams. A real key is to begin to see your obstacles the way God sees them. In order to do this, you must see with eyes of faith. Many in the Bible did, and because they did, they saw great dreams manifest.

The children of Israel looked at the Red Sea through eyes of fear. They saw an obstacle, Moses saw an opportunity, and they all walked across on dry ground. Obstacles move when you see them as opportunities.

When the Israelite army saw the champion of the Philistines named Goliath, they viewed a GIANT obstacle. A young teenager saw a GIANT opportunity. David won an indescribable victory! Giant obstacles fall when you see them as giant opportunities.

When the disciples of Christ saw a cross on Golgotha, they saw a murderous obstacle, but Jesus saw matchless opportunity. Salvation, healing, breakthrough, and miracles manifest when you see obstacles as opportunities.

Joseph was a man who had the ability to change obstacles into opportunities. Whether it was in Potiphar's house or the prison house, Joseph made the most of every moment.

You will overcome dream-killing obstacles when you view them as opportunities.

5. Never quit on your dream.

Quitting is the ultimate dream killer. No dream that was quit on ever came true. When you quit on a dream, you have unleashed finality in your life. When you quit, you are declaring, "It's over. I'm through and my dream is done." In order to see your dreams come true, you are going to have to purpose something very powerful in your own mind and heart: *quit quitting.*

In the most intense times you must learn how to persevere and refuse to give up on your dreams. Let me give you a few incentives that will inspire you not to quit on your dreams no matter what.

The pain you're in now is nothing compared to the pain of quitting.

The pain you are facing right now does not even come close to the pain of quitting. I think to live with the pain of what might have been or what could have been far exceeds the pain of quitting. If you quit on your dream, you will always wonder what if?

You're probably thinking, "What if my dream doesn't come true?" My question to you is...what if it does?

Vince Lombardi said, "Once you learn to quit, it becomes a habit."

Never allow yourself to develop the habit of quitting. Have you ever known people who seemed to be addicted to quitting? You must never let that become you.

Refuse to allow your mentality to become one of a quitter. In my life and ministry I have wrestled many times with wanting to quit. But I did not, because that's not who I want to be, nor is it who God has called me to be.

God has not called you to be a quitter either. A God-birthed dream will require you to get addicted to trying, not quitting.

Try again.

Try something different.

Try to never stop trying.

Trying is habit-forming; get hooked on trying, and you will see your dreams come to pass!

The only thing that will guarantee your dream will die is quitting.

Once you quit, your dream is dead. But as long as you are still trying, your dream is alive. If you are reading this and are thinking, "It's too late; I have already killed my dream because I quit," I want to tell you what I believe. I believe the Lord is allowing you to read this book at this precise moment because it is time to give your dream another shot.

When you make up your mind to do that, you are breathing new life into your dream and resuscitating your God-ordained destiny.

Losers quit when they are tired; winners quit when the job is done.

Don't allow being tired to cause you to quit. My grandfather was an amazing man. He preached the gospel for more than sixty years. He passed away at eighty-three years of age in the pulpit! What a way to go. He died doing what he loved to do. He used to say, "I would rather wear out than rust out!" Quite honestly, you don't have to wear out or rust out. God is full of grace, and He will give you peace and strength to not quit.

Use wisdom, rest, revive, and rejuvenate, but whatever you do, mighty dreamer, don't quit! You are a winner, and winners do get tired; they just don't quit.

I am sure that many times Joseph felt like quitting. There must have been long seasons where he had to focus and trust with all his might that his dreams would come to pass. Somehow he did, and everything God showed him became a reality.

Doing nothing will kill your dream every time.

Your dreams will come to pass when you defeat the dream killer of quitting. The enemy is frustrated with many of you right now as you read this book. You have decided, "Today is the day I QUIT QUITTING!"

6. Go from dreaming to doing.

It is amazingly important that your dreams don't die because you did nothing to ensure that they would come to pass.

Doing nothing will kill your dream every time.

You must do something. Your dream will require you to do something. The apostle Paul had an incredible understanding of this.

It's not enough to be a great dreamer; you must also become a great doer. Not only was Paul a dreamer, but he was also a doer. He dreamed of making an incredible impact, and he did it. He dreamed of establishing powerful churches to propagate the gospel, and he did. He dreamed of being a part of a revival that would sweep the world, and he did it!

The greatest dreamers must become the greatest doers.

- Noah was a doer.

- Abraham was a doer.

- Joseph was a doer.

- David was a doer.

- Jesus was a doer.

Listen to these incredible words written by James.

> But don't just listen to God's word. You must do what it says. Otherwise, you are only fooling yourselves.
> —JAMES 1:22, NLT

If all you ever do is dream but never do, you are fooling yourself. Your great dream will require great action. The New King James Version says, "Be doers of the word..." The word *doers* comes from an incredible Greek word, *poietes*. It means to be a performer and a producer. A dream is nothing if it is not produced and performed. God has given you great dreams that they may be produced and performed!

The graveyard is full of great dreams. I say that because I'm sure there have been many people who have had incredible dreams, but when they died, their dreams died along with them. All because they never moved from dreaming to doing. Don't take your dreams to the grave with you. Do everything God has called you to do in this life!

You must take action, produce, and perform in order for your dreams to become reality!

7. Apply the six principles you just learned!

During the process of pursuing your dream you must apply each one of these principles. When you do, you will see your dreams become reality. God will give you the victory, and He will get the glory!

Power Prayer

Pray this prayer now:

> *Father God, You are the great dream giver. Thank You for my dreams. Thank You that I have all I need to bring to pass the dream You gave me.*
>
> *Lord, please enable me to be flexible in difficult times. Cause me to see the bigger picture and never to be bound by pride.*
>
> *Precious Lord, help me to be motivated by faith rather than imprisoned by fear. My faith honors You, Mighty God. In hard times, may I continually walk by faith and not by sight.*
>
> *Mighty Redeemer, help me to get over what's over. Never allow me to hold anything from the past that would hinder Your work in me today or sabotage my dreams for tomorrow.*
>
> *Strength-giving Jesus, I bless Your name and declare that I do not quit. I confess in faith that I will pursue and press on in Your power to see the dreams You have given me manifest. I shall run and not grow weary; I shall walk and not faint.*
>
> *God of all times, thank You for the ability not just to dream the dream but also to do the dream. I will not*

miss out on my dream becoming a reality because I would not be a doer. Lord, I will perform and produce the dream, and I thank You that You will perform and produce Your word. These all will come together. Then the unstoppable and supernatural manifestation of my dreams will take place. The power of every dream killer in my life is broken in the mighty name of Jesus! Thank You, Lord, that the dream and the dreamer not only survive but also thrive!

I apply these principles and move forward in victory. I now anticipate the mighty fulfillment of my dreams! In Jesus's mighty name, amen!

Notes

CHAPTER 1
DARE TO DREAM BIG

1.   TheLifeCoach.com, "Michael Jordan's Secrets of Success," http://www.thelifecoach.com/881/michael-jordans-secrets-success/ (accessed June 14, 2013).

2.   Charles F. Pfieffer, Howard F. Vos, and John Rea, eds., *Wycliffe Bible Dictionary* (Peabody, MA: Hendrickson Publishers, 1998), s.v. "Joseph."

3.   National Aviation Hall of Fame, "Herb Kelleher," http://www.nationalaviation.org/kelleher-herbert/ (accessed June 14, 2013).

4.   ThinkExist.com, "Pablo Picasso Quotes," http://thinkexist.com/quotation/everything_you_can_imagine_is_real/143235.html (accessed June 14, 2013).

CHAPTER 2
THE POWER OF A DREAM

1.   ThinkExist.com, "Walt Disney Quotes," http://thinkexist.com/quotation/if_you_can_dream_it-you_can_do_it-always_remember/226638.html (accessed June 14, 2013).

2.   WaltDisneyCompany.com, "The Walt Disney Company Reports Fourth Quarter and Full Year Earnings for Fiscal 2012," press release, November 8, 2012, http://thewaltdisneycompany.com/sites/default/files/reports/q4-fy12-earnings.pdf (accessed June 14, 2013).

3.   ThinkExist.com, "C. S. Lewis Quotes," http://thinkexist.com/quotation/you_are_never_too_old_to_set_another_goal_or_to/201591.html (accessed June 14, 2013).

CHAPTER 7
CHARACTER ASSASSINATION

1.   Sharon J. Huntington, "From Shells and Spice to Shekels and Mites," *Christian Science Monitor*, November 25, 2003, http://www.csmonitor.com/2003/1125/p14s02-hfks.html (accessed June 14, 2013).

2.   Merriam-Webster.com, s.v. "undervalue," http://www.merriam-webster.com/dictionary/undervalue (accessed June 14, 2013).

3.   Pfieffer, Vos, and Rea, eds., *Wycliffe Bible Dictionary*, s.v. "Midian."

CHAPTER 10
READY FOR A SETUP

1.   Nahum M. Sarna, *The JPS Torah Commentary: Genesis* (Jerusalem: The Jewish Publication Society, 1989), 121.

CHAPTER 13
THE BONDAGE OF BITTERNESS

1.   William D. Mounce, *The Analytical Lexicon to the Greek New Testament* (Grand Rapids, MI: Zondervan Publishing Company, 1993), 207.

2.   ThinkExist.com, "Lewis B. Smedes Quotes," http://thinkexist .com/quotation/to_forgive_is_to_set_a_prisoner_free_and_discover/ 214491.html (accessed June 17, 2013).

To contact Pastor Raley, you can reach him via the following ways:

Twitter: @pastorraley

Facebook: Jim Raley like page

Instagram: @pastorraley

Websites: www.jimraley.com or www.calvaryfl.com

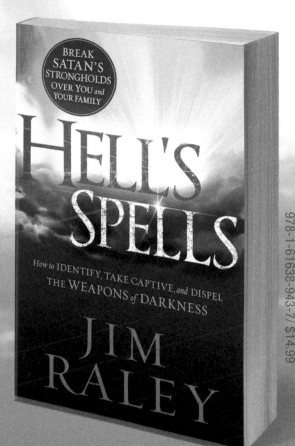